The Clicked Retriever

Lana Mitchell　CLICK! for Success Dog Training

The Clicked Retriever

Lana R. Mitchell

Distributed by:
Dogwise Publishing
A Division of Direct Book Service, Inc.
PO Box 2778
701B Poplar
Wenatchee, Washington 98807
1-509-663-9115, 1-800-776-2665
website: www.dogwisepublishing.com
email: info@dogwisepublshing.com

Limits of Liability and Disclaimer of Warranty:
The author and publisher shall not be liable in the event of incidental or consequential damages in connection with, or arising out of, the furnishing, performance, or use of the instructions and suggestions contained in this book.

Photos by Lana Mitchell

Cataloging-in-Publication Data is available upon request from the Library of Congress.

Printed in the U.S.A.

FOREWORD

I was taking a traditional obedience training program for AKC open class with about 20 other students over several weeks. Things were going okay for me until we got to the retrieve exercise. The instructor started to explain to the class that we would be using the "ear pinch" method. I was not feeling very good about this and it got worse after he explained the details.

I was determined to find another approach that did not require an aversive. I found a couple of great trainers certified by APDT that helped me hone my clicker skills and then one of these trainers told me about the book *The Clicked Retriever* by Lana Mitchell. I found what may have been the last used book on the market since it was out of print at that time.

I began following Lana's detailed step by step approach to teaching a retrieve based on using a clicker and positive reinforcement. I was very impressed with Lana's logical and detailed approached. It was also amazing to me that as I would read and practice a question would come to mind and in the next paragraph she anticipated my question and provided an answer. It is quite clear that Lana has done much research and taught this method before committing it to book form.

I felt it would be a terrible loss to the world of dog training for this work to remain out of print; not only because of the specific example of a positive retrieve method, but also because of Lana's great instructional writing style (I wish more books were available in this style.) Anyway sometime after myself and other Lana Mitchell fans asked Dogwise to bring back this wonderful book I was excited to hear that they had decided to publish it. So I have to add that I was impressed that Dogwise really listens to their customers!

My dog ended up doing his retrieve as well as the top 3 or 4 dogs in our class and didn't have his ears pinched.

Thanks Lana and thanks Dogwise!

Wes Anderson & "TD"
Click! for Success student and dog

TABLE OF CONTENTS

INDEX OF FIGURES

INTRODUCTION

This book in its earlier editions helped a lot of trainers not only shape a reliable retrieve chain, but also helped solve many retrieve problems. This newest edition is more concise, with a totally revised Clicker Training Introduction section.

The Clicked Retriever is really three books in one. Section 1, "Clicker Training Introduction," contains information for a novice trainer to learn about operant conditioning training and how to effectively use a behavior marker—usually a clicker. It explains the advantages of using operant conditioning over some of the more popular and better-known training methods, and why a behavior marker helps a dog and trainer team reach their full potential.

Section 2, "Understanding the Retrieve Elements" is as much information about the many behaviors that are included in the retrieve chain as anyone can possibly absorb. It explains the necessary elements for the AKC Retrieve on the Flat and Retrieve over High Jump classes and how the exercises are scored. There is a chapter on sizing dumbbells and the importance of choosing the correct size and type for your dog. It contains a study on how chains are formed, and many photographs showing dogs executing the individual behaviors and explanations of how they should be shaped.

Section 3, "The Retrieve Workbook, Shaping the Retrieve Elements" explains in depth how to shape each behavior in the retrieve chain. The workbook section is a step-by-step guide to teaching the retrieve from the first look at the dumbbell to executing front and gives behaviors. It contains detailed chapters about shaping your dog to perform all required behaviors in the AKC Directed Retrieve and Scent Discrimination exercises. Also in this section is information on applying the techniques taught in this book to the sport of Flyball and to retrieving skills needed by Service Dogs.

The Clicked Retriever will help you and your dog enjoy the retrieve training experience, and you will enjoy watching, as your best friend becomes a clicker-trained dog.

Lana Mitchell

SECTION 1

CLICKER
TRAINING
INTRODUCTION

1 - 1 GETTING STARTED

RECOMMENDED TRAINING EQUIPMENT

- ✓ A well-fitting non-correcting collar – the soft cloth type with a plastic clip closure is an excellent choice.

- ✓ Lightweight leashes of 2', 4' and 6' lengths.

- ✓ A lightweight long line if needed. Retractable leashes are not recommended since they make a clicking sound when the brake button is depressed and confusion between the clicker and the brake is possible.

- ✓ Two dumbbells made of lightweight wood. An exact description can be found in Section 3.

- ✓ Favorite treats – wieners (hot dogs), liver, lunchmeat, or anything else the dog will work for that can be quickly swallowed with minimal chewing.

- ✓ A Clicker - the wrist and finger clickers are convenient and always close at hand.

- ✓ A sense of humor, an open and creative mind, a distraction-free work area, and a hungry, alert dog.

OPERANT CONDITIONING - EXPLAINED

Since time began, operant conditioning has been the basis by which all animals, man included, have learned to fend for themselves—by repeating behaviors that had favorable results and eliminating those that did not. Another term for operant conditioning could be "process of elimination." Any behavior that does not return a benefit of some sort is eliminated and only those behaviors that give favorable results are repeated.

Operant Conditioning training is the act of reinforcing any and all desired behaviors that a dog offers so that he will offer them again. Ignoring any and all undesired behaviors the dog offers so that he will not offer them again is a useful tool when using this method.

If a dog trainer eliminates everything that doesn't look like the behavior he wants, all that remains for the dog to offer is the desired behavior. In other words, if a trainer who is shaping a <u>sit</u> behavior extinguishes (fails to reinforce) all offered behaviors that are not a <u>sit</u> behavior, his dog will repeatedly offer the <u>sit</u> behavior—the desired behavior. Furthermore, he will stop offering all behaviors that are not sits, since they do not give favorable results. The dog will eventually extinguish non-reinforced behaviors when he is expected to <u>sit</u>.

For a moment think what could happen if each occurrence of undesired behavior were to be punished rather than ignored? Once acclimated to a punishment method of training, animals seldom offer behaviors. For years, competition trainers have believed the use of compulsion was required; that teaching animals to work to avoid punishment makes training go more quickly. Many of today's trainers use a gentler method like Clicker Training for simple behaviors, but then revert to punishment methods for the more advanced behaviors. They lack an understanding of how to use Clicker Training to fine-tune simple behaviors into the complex behavior chains required for competition.

Regardless of whether the behavior is a simple sit or a complex chain, marking each behavior the instant it happens will make it a memorable experience for the dog. This in turn ensures he will have a desire to repeat the experience. As a dog gives up undesired behaviors, his trainer can begin to refine each occurrence of the desired behaviors until it can be perfectly performed.

Not all behaviors that we desire from our dogs are freely offered. Those that are not offered may be induced or encouraged. They are reinforced in the same way that freely offered behaviors are reinforced, but with a little help to get them started. For instance, if a dog turns to the left because a treat was tossed in that direction and he is then reinforced for looking or moving in that direction, it is an induced behavior. There's nothing wrong with that and I recommend it to help training go faster for the dog and easier for the trainer.

THE CLICKER

The clicker is our conditioned reinforcer - our behavior marker. Its role is to mark the exact part of the behavior for which a dog will be fed a treat or given a reward of his choice. The entire action of marking and treating a behavior is what is meant by the terms "reinforce," "reinforcement," and "R+" throughout this book. To reinforce a dog is to click and treat him.

The clicker means a treat, a special morsel of food that the dog loves, has been earned. The clicker is the one constant in Clicker Training, and is a very powerful tool. Clicking without treating will cause the clicker to lose its power and will slow your dog's progress.

What the dog is doing when the click is heard is the most important element in Clicker Training. In teaching a dog the recall, for instance, clicking only when he is traveling at a fast gait will change the behavior from a recall to a fast recall. By clicking him at the right time, he learns that speed is a desired element of the recall behavior. When he hears the click he will continue to come at that pace and might even speed up to get his treat. By always marking the recall when he is traveling at his fastest, and ignoring slow recalls, he develops a desire to travel fast whenever the recall command is given.

In early training, the sound of the clicker will always abort whatever behavior the dog is engaged in when he hears it. Later, however, the clicker is used to test the dog's understanding of the entire behavior – his "fluency." It becomes a proofing tool that, while being faded becomes a measuring tool of the dog's fluency.

1 - 2 THE SHAPING PROCESS

SHAPING IS -

Shaping is the reinforcing of a behavior that is being offered so that it will be offered more often.

All dogs naturally know how to sit, down, bark, stand and carry things. We shape them so they will perform these simple behaviors only when a particular command has been given them. That command, called the "conditioned stimulus," will one day cause the dog to perform a specific behavior. Looking at this from the dog's point of view, we could say that the <u>dog</u> is doing the shaping. He is learning which behavior is the stimulus control that causes the trainer to click and treat him.

Although clicker training affords the trainer much leeway, there are particular rules that, when followed, will increase the dog's reliability and understanding.

It is not always necessary to have a specific behavior in mind to start a shaping session. Just grab a clicker and some treats, allow the dog to offer some behaviors, and start clicking one you would like to see repeated. I start out with the spin, wave bye-bye, go to bed, say prayers, walk beside me, look at me, be quiet, bow, and other fun behaviors to build a learning base before going on to serious training.

Even when shaping "trick" behaviors, think of them as the training base upon which an OTCh (Obedience Trial Champion) dog may be created. Think of his early training as the foundation upon which all other training will be piled. Without a solid foundation of knowing how to learn and respond to cues, the dog does not possess the prerequisites for becoming a reliably trained dog, and will have a difficult if not impossible time moving on to advanced work and complex behavior chains.

YOUR DOG -

You and your dog are in for a wonderful experience, as you both become familiar with the power of the clicker. Your dog, after becoming familiar with clicker training, will begin offering new behaviors for every event in his life. There are few rules to clicker training; just be ready to reinforce any cute new behaviors and build a repertoire of both tricks and functional household tasks. The more you teach your dog the faster he will learn new behaviors. The clicker also makes extinguishing unwanted behaviors go more smoothly because the dog is more willing to give them up.

Clicker training works best with food-motivated dogs. If your dog is not food motivated, you will want to find the one thing he will do just about anything to get and use that as a food substitute. Another solution is to increase your dog's food drive through the help of an experienced trainer who uses positive methods.

1 - 3 THE TEN LAWS OF SHAPING

FROM DON'T SHOOT THE DOG!

by Karen Pryor, used with author's permission

1. Raise criteria in increments small enough so that the subject always has a realistic chance for reinforcement.

2. Train one thing at a time; don't try to shape for two criteria simultaneously.

3. Always put the current level of response onto a variable schedule of reinforcement before adding or raising criteria.

4. When introducing a new criterion, temporarily relax the old ones.

5. Stay ahead of your subject. Plan your shaping program completely so that if the subject makes sudden progress you are aware of what to reinforce next.

6. Don't change trainers in midstream; you can have several trainers per subject, but stick to one shaper per behavior.

7. If one shaping procedure is not eliciting progress, find another; there are as many ways to get behavior, as there are trainers to think them up.

8. Don't interrupt a training session gratuitously; that constitutes a punishment.

9. If a behavior deteriorates, review the shaping.

10. Quit while you're ahead.

THE LAWS OF SHAPING, EXPLAINED

To assist with your understanding of Karen's shaping laws I have included my own explanation of each.

1. Raising criteria to a level higher than the subject has the ability to perform can cause the behavior to break down. The smaller the increments the better chance the trainer and dog have of success. The speed with which a trainer may raise criteria is not a function of his subject's ability, but a measure of how well he and the dog are communicating within the shaping process. It is important to watch for feedback from the dog, raising criteria when he displays a full understanding and willingness to give more, and lowering it any time he seems confused or stressed.

2. A single reinforcement cannot convey two pieces of information for the dog. Shaping for a <u>straight</u> sit at heel position, for instance, should not be combined with shaping for a <u>fast</u> sit at heel position. They should be shaped separately, and the speed criterion added after straight has been established. In turn, speed will need some work as the straight criterion becomes solid. When the two behaviors have been shaped to perfection, they will combine naturally.

3. Once a behavior is learned, it should be reinforced only occasionally by placing it on a variable reinforcement schedule to maintain it at its present level.

4. What is once learned is not forgotten, but under the pressure of having to perform an old behavior with new criteria, the already known behavior can temporarily fall apart. For this reason, present standards must be lowered in preparation for adding new criteria to a known behavior. A fast recall could become slower after either the stay/wait command or a front has been added, but speed will be restored when the dog accepts the new criteria.

5. Shaping "breakthroughs" can happen at any time. It can be somewhat of a shock to see a dog suddenly go beyond the step currently being shaped, so plan ahead and be prepared to reinforce these sudden improvements.

6. Trainers have different standards, reaction times, and expectations of progress. When a new trainer takes over in mid-shaping, the subject is not reinforced until the new trainers' differences are accommodated, constituting possible corrections in the dog's mind. When shaping a particular behavior, see it through to the end if possible. If one trainer isn't communicating with the dog, end the session, give the dog a short break, and then begin later with the new trainer.

7. There are many ways to encourage proper responses from a subject, and creativity is a key element. When a subject doesn't understand a behavior, it is time for the trainer to try other approaches until the subject responds.

8. Ending a shaping session for conversation or other non-training activity leaves a dog hanging, not knowing if this is still training or not. Always have a definite start and end to all training sessions as well as all exercises. Your dog will develop crispness to his performance that comes only from a clear understanding of what is expected.

9. When a behavior deteriorates, simply return to kindergarten with your dog. Quickly review the entire shaping process with a series of easy reinforcements.

10. The length of any shaping session depends upon the attention span of the dog. Training sessions should terminate on a high note, after progress has been achieved. My rule of thumb is to make training sessions like a book the reader doesn't wish to put down. Quitting a shaping session while a dog is performing at his best will cause him to begin his next shaping session with the same enthusiasm he felt when he had to quit the previous game.

ADDITIONAL RULES

The more tools the trainer has, the more "tricks" he can pull out of his "magic bag," the more successful he and his dog will be. So, here are a few more helpful rules, bringing the list to 16:

1.   Keep training sessions short and frequent.

2.   Introduce a cue only after a behavior exists. (There are a handful of behaviors where the command is added while the behavior is being shaped.)

3.   Allowing the dog to learn on his own by experiencing which behaviors are reinforceable and which are not eliminates any need for corrective measures.

4.   When behaviors contained in a chain are asked for outside the chain, they should be reinforced on a variable schedule.

5.   Always start with accuracy, and then raise criteria in small but measurable increments, i.e., distraction, distance, and duration - the 3 Ds.

6.   Raising the speed criterion may effectively be done only after all other criteria have been shaped. To do so earlier will, at the least, deteriorate accuracy.

1 - 4 THE TRAINING GAME

HOW IT WORKS

To play the game with people, choose a behavior that can be easily performed while remaining in one place, such as touching one's head or raising an arm. When your subject performs anything close to your chosen behavior, click and treat (reward with chocolate or promises to wash dishes). Work on your timing, for if you click too late you will realize it by the third click; your subject's behavior will tell you. When this happens, abort the training exercise and start over with a new behavior and click earlier. Before quitting the game, ensure the subject understands which behavior he is being trained to perform.

When playing the game with your dog, the dog will stop what he is doing when he hears the click and will return to you for the treat. This is an important element of the shaping process. The clicker means that the behavior is over and it is time to get paid. This aborting of the behavior enables the dog to restart, to re-offer the behavior from scratch. Tossing the treat a distance away will help to abort stationary behaviors such as sits and downs. By allowing him to re-offer the behavior (restart the game) you can gauge your dog's understanding and willingness to perform it.

Practice adding commands and signals for simple behaviors like shaking hands, walking backwards, and spinning. Again, work on your timing, as this is the most critical element in all training methods.

BE PREPARED

Before a specific behavior can be shaped to completion, a clear picture of the final outcome must be in the trainer's mind. Only when the trainer has a mental picture of how the behavior will look when complete can she shape for it.

It is important that you be ready to reinforce sudden bursts of greatness from the dog. A puppy that has been lured into a sit may suddenly offer the sit on his own. The prepared trainer who reinforces that sit will be leaps ahead of where he was a moment ago. Having missed the opportunity, the unprepared trainer might not see the sit offered again for some time.

During the clicker training process dogs are experimenting with behaviors, offering first this and then that, hoping one will elicit a click from the trainer. A dog that suddenly thinks he's got it will offer the behavior he thinks *it* is. If the trainer is not quick to see *it,* the dog might assume that's not *it* and will go on to offer something else. Anyone who has been the training subject in the training game can remember how that felt. Anyone who has played the training game as the trainer knows how easy it is to miss an opportunity to click, especially when the subject offered several behaviors in quick succession.

DOGS THAT QUIT

There could be a variety of reasons for your dog to lose interest in you or the training game during a shaping session. He could be in what is called a learning dip (explained later), you could be boring him, in which case you need to add some excitement to the game; or he could have a full tummy, a common problem with puppies. After raising the distraction criterion dogs often seem disinterested, which is a good reason why distractions are added in the smallest of increments.

THE PRIMARY REINFORCER

The primary reinforcer is what the dog is working to get; it is the "pay" for which dogs perform. Dogs that readily perform a sit in the kitchen for a bit of cracker will require a more desirable treat to perform the same behavior in the presence of distractions. Grilled chicken, sautéed chicken hearts, or calves liver cooked with garlic will bring most dogs around. Because the pay must be adequate for the dog to perform, study your dog's reactions to certain treats. If your dog prefers cheese to steak, use cheese to reinforce difficult behaviors like heeling past another dog without looking at him.

ABOUT TRAINING WITH TREATS

Treats must not be so important to the dog that they totally rule his behavior. I start out by having the treats visible, but not handy. They are in a container on a table, or shelf, or on the floor to one side. The dog learns that he gets only what has been earned. Like bank tellers who don't just take money home when they want some, but wait for Friday and accept a paycheck for the amount earned rather than the entire contents of the bank's vault, dogs learn moderation and that a treat not earned is a treat not given to them.

Having the treats in a bowl near the dog and removing the bowl each time he dives at it will eventually extinguish his "if I can see food it's mine" way of thinking. You can be trained to give him treats, and once he learns that fact will put effort into finding the right behaviors that cause you to click and treat him rather than trying to snitch the treats from the bowl.

JACKPOTS

Jackpots are bonus treats for a job well done. Giving jackpots is a form of variable reinforcement. Giving special or larger than normal treats can intensify the dog's willingness to work. I give jackpots when the dog has surpassed my expectations, has mastered a particularly tough part of a behavior, has gotten over a slump that seemed to last forever, or is making an effort to get back into the game after he had quit playing. Receiving a jackpot makes any event more memorable to the dog.

Jackpots don't have to be treats but could be a game of tug, a Frisbee™ chase, or a ride in the car to the park or ice cream stand.

THE TRAINING "W"

There are two separate incidents that take place during the shaping process where known, reinforceable behavior is voluntarily abandoned by the dog. It can happen at any time throughout the shaping process, but is seen most often during initial shaping phases. The Training "W" is so consistent that an experienced trainer can easily see it coming and can prepare for it.

The Training "W" contains two distinct dips, which occur with people, with horses, and most certainly with dogs. It usually happens just about the time the trainer is thinking, "This is easy." One can emerge from these learning dips unscathed by doing nothing more than waiting them out. Knowing that it is possible and common for dogs to voluntarily, albeit temporarily, extinguish reinforceable behaviors throughout the shaping process will help the trainer accept it when it occurs.

The first dip in the Training "W" should be an exciting time for the trainer, as it is the dog's signal that he is on the verge of understanding a new behavior. During this dip the dog stops offering the behavior for which he has been most recently reinforced and offers other known behaviors instead. He may also spend some time staring at the treat or the trainer or he might wander off, but not too far if he is on a leash. If the trainer waits, the dog will attempt the behavior, receive his reinforcement, and resume the game with renewed interest and determination.

One cannot afford the luxury of feeling as though the shaping dragon has been slain however; the second dip of the Training "W" will usually follow within minutes of the first.

At the onset of the second dip, the dog looks as though he is suddenly flooded with the realization that he has been getting paid for working. He can look at, bite at, or dig at the clicker and go for the hand or dish holding the treats. He sometimes offers other known behaviors but will more often stand and stare at the trainer and at the treat. He appears to be waiting for the trainer to give in and treat him for doing nothing. Again, if the trainer is patient and waits, the dog will return to offering the behavior with renewed interest.

It is recommended that after the second dip the trainer continue working only long enough to be offered several good responses, perhaps with one slight rise in criteria. Stopping with the dog working hard will cause him to begin the next training session with the determination and enthusiasm of a dog feeling confident about his role.

I once heard Diane Baumann say that a good trainer does not hesitate to put the leash back on the dog. What she meant is that a successful trainer is one who will retrain an area that is not perfect rather than to go on. In the same manner, a clicker trainer does not feel defeated when a dog stops offering a behavior, but instead waits to see what the dog will do next, lowering criteria and retracing steps if needed. Missed steps in any training program are equal to no training at all.

16

HELPING THE DOG

Avoid helping the dog verbally or physically. This might be a *training* game to you, but it's a *thinking* game to your dog. Any words of encouragement constitute a distraction – keep quiet and smile a lot.

On that same subject, no amount of saying, "Sit!" is going to enhance the dog's behavior while shaping a <u>sit</u>. Leaning closer to the dog's ear or speaking in a louder voice will have similar results. Waiting for the dog to perform the <u>sit</u> on his own and then letting him know that it was correct, however, not only allows him to offer the behavior, but also significantly reduces the required training time.

1 - 5 RAISING CRITERIA

WHY RAISE IT?

If demands for better performance are never pressed, better performance will never be offered. Withholding the click and waiting for the behavior to change slightly can accomplish increases in criteria. By clicking only for changes that will lead to perfection in the execution of the behavior, and then raising each criterion in the smallest of increments, the trainer is able to shape each nuance of a given behavior. Just clicking a dog for looking at a dumbbell, for instance, will never become a retrieve no matter how many years you spend doing it.

ADVICE FOR RAISING CRITERIA

- ✓ Raise one criterion at a time.

- ✓ Raise it only in one measurable increment at a time such as duration, distance, intensity, distraction, or speed.

- ✓ When raising criterion in any category, already established criteria must be relaxed.

- ✓ Reinforcements should always be given for any higher level of performance.

- ✓ Ignore new behaviors the dog offers unless it's something great like walking on his front paws.

- ✓ Be prepared to reinforce sudden improvements in performance or bursts of understanding.

- ✓ Keep in mind that withholding or delaying reinforcement will either intensify or extinguish already known and previously reinforced behavior.

When in doubt, animals usually return to what they learned first or what was last reinforced. To prevent digression to a previously reinforced behavior, remember to raise each criterion individually and in measurable increments, such as farther, longer, or with one more distraction. If your dog returns to some non-related behavior while in a shaping session, it's an indication that you probably moved too fast.

Anytime a behavior deteriorates while attempting to raise a criterion, lower it again and reinforce the behavior several times at the previous level before attempting to raise the criterion again. By giving several reinforcements for the behavior at the dog's success level, he will be brought back into the game without stress and will be more willing to try the behavior with the new criterion added. Always keep in mind that the dog will not stay in the training game unless he is winning on a regular basis. It is the trainer's role to keep criteria at attainable levels, and increase them only in increments that enable the dog's success.

SUCCESSIVE APPROXIMATION

When reinforcement for a known behavior is withheld, the dog will offer an exaggerated version of the behavior. The new behavior now becomes the behavior that will be reinforced; previous levels of the same behavior will no longer be reinforced.

This is one of the most significant differences between training by operant conditioning and some of the more conventional dog training methods. It is not necessary for the clicker trainer to see a complete behavior to reinforce it; for any part of it to become the new reinforceable behavior.

Clicking "Ghost" Behaviors

Learning dogs are often performing the behavior in their minds long before their bodies are capable of it.

In the dog's mind he might actually be thinking of downing even though he's not really in a downed position. His body language will indicate his thoughts, and those thoughts can be reinforced and ignored the same as a physical response can. The more a dog is reinforced for thinking of downing the more likely he is to perform the down behavior.

So, how does the trainer know what the dog is thinking? When he drops his head, he's thinking of downing. When he's placing one foot out while dropping his head he's thinking more about downing, and so on. By clicking each variance in the behavior of downing, even the most macho dog will eventually lie down and allow a tummy rub.

My own student trainers learn to teach the down by luring with treats from a point above the dog's mouth to between his front feet, clicking each time the dog drops his head. When the dog understands that dropping his head is a reinforceable behavior, the trainer raises criteria by no longer reinforcing a head drop. When the dog again offers the head down behavior and it is not reinforced, he will put more effort into the dropping of the head, which will cause another change in his posture, such as a foot forward and a shoulder drop. Since this behavior is closer to a down than the previous behavior, it is reinforced and becomes the new reinforceable behavior.

VARIABLE REINFORCEMENT

Variable reinforcement is the very crux of enabling a behavior-shaping program to progress into a perfectly executed on-cue behavior.

Reinforcing every occurrence of a behavior can cause it to deteriorate into a variation of the originally shaped behavior, while requiring the dog to perform a behavior two or more times for a single reinforcement will help to keep the behavior at its present level.

Variable reinforcement scheduling will also allow the trainer to selectively reinforce only the best of the behaviors as they are offered. For instance, if the most crooked sits at front are ignored and only more correct sits are reinforced, the dog will elect to give the straighter sits. With this schedule the trainer can eliminate all but perfectly straight fronts and is able to move on to reinforcing fast fronts, centered fronts, or good fronts with distractions present.

When a behavior is shaped to perfection, continuing to reinforce it only occasionally will maintain it at its present level. Withholding reinforcement for more than one occurrence of a behavior will generally cause the dog to exaggerate the behavior by going faster or higher.

To clarify this point, here is an example: A dog is repeatedly walking to a target, being clicked, and returning to the trainer for the treat. When the clicker is withheld for a touch, the dog automatically returns after touching because that's what he's always done, even though there was no click. He hesitates, waits for his treat, and not getting one, returns to perform another touch. Often, he'll return at a faster pace having more determination because he wasn't reinforced for his previous behavior.

By clicking the second behavior, the trainer has captured a faster performance and can soon raise his expectations to include the faster speed criterion.

1 - 6 THE TRAINING GAME

Train Often

- ✓ Ideally, dogs should be trained in as many short sessions as possible. Three training sessions per day is a good schedule, while five to ten is best.

- ✓ There is no minimum training time but the maximum should be 10 minutes for a novice dog, longer for a more experienced dog.

- ✓ When beginning to shape a behavior as difficult as the take, keep training sessions under three minutes giving the dog an opportunity to be reinforced many times but not wearing him out on it.

Remain Quiet

- ✓ Verbally cueing the dog cannot trigger unknown behavior.

- ✓ Cheering the dog on with words of encouragement can present enough distraction to bring work to an abrupt halt.

Remain Calm

- ✓ Frustration on the part of the trainer will cause the dog to quit working and learning.

- ✓ Frustration in the dog, however, can lead to brilliance and creativity.

- ✓ If training isn't progressing, lower your criteria and reinforce an already known behavior several times. If the dog seems interested after reinforcing the lesser behavior a few times, try the new behavior again and then quit if you get it.

Move Ahead

- ✓ When beginning to shape a new behavior or any time criteria are raised for a known behavior, be prepared to lower overall criteria a bit so the dog can win. So, if the dog quits fronting on a recall because you've put demands on it, go back to a fronting game to get his mind back on working for pay.

- ✓ Be ready to reinforce moments of genius with a jackpot. Jackpots don't always have to be treats, especially if there was a tense moment for the dog. I often toss out a ball or a tug toy and play for a few minutes before resuming work or quitting that session.

Maintain Good Training Habits

- ✓ Know your dog's limitations. Watch for signs of stress and be prepared to lighten the training load.

- ✓ Be aware of distractions, stopping the session if distractions are influencing the dog's willingness to work; move to a new location and begin again starting with lowered criteria.

- ✓ Always end a training session on a good note even if to do so requires lowering the criteria you have already set for a given behavior. Keep your standards flexible.

- ✓ Quit a session before your dog quits on you by ending training sessions with the dog wanting o do more. Be like a good book and always leave your dog wanting to "read just one more page."

- ✓ Training too fast, even though the dog appears to be able to handle it, could lead to serious training problems later. Take care not to skim over important lessons; training "holes" that will turn up later when they can be more difficult to overcome could result.

- ✓ Enjoy watching undesirable behaviors that are extremely cute. If you think you will never recapture them, go ahead and click! You can always return to your present lesson after getting that chance behavior on cue.

LATENT LEARNING

Latent learning occurs between training sessions. A mental picture of the last thing the dog does during a training session will stay with him until the next session, as will any resulting emotions. Quitting on a good note will often cause a dog to enter into the next training session with seemingly accelerated willingness and understanding, because that is how the previous training session ended. Ending a training session during a learning dip will almost guarantee that is how the next training session will begin - in a learning dip.

CORRECTIONS

Avoid corrections, either verbal or physical when shaping new behaviors. Correcting a dog for not learning a new behavior holds an air of unfairness and stifles his willingness to be creative. The dog could be exhibiting unwanted behavior while thinking of giving you the very behavior you want. A reprimand at this time could result in a learning set back.

As dogs become fluent at performing a behavior, adding a mild aversive for any non-compliance is acceptable. Turning your back on the dog for several seconds before resuming training or issuing a verbal aversive is usually enough for the truly clicker trained dog. "Uh-oh" and "Icky" are my favorite verbal reprimands.

The best "correction" for conveying that the dog's performance was not up to current criteria levels is to turn away. When the dog, expecting a click/treat response is given the trainer's back instead, he instantly understands that no reinforcement is coming. A dog that understands how the operant conditioning game works will immediately try to get the trainer's attention and offer a behavior. It might not be the one he was previously working on, but he's in the game and is trying his best to figure it all out.

Soon, the dog understands the back-turn completely and when corrected in this manner goes on to offer the desired behavior, often accelerated with higher criteria.

CONSEQUENCES

Consequences, positive and negative, may take many forms. The positive consequence is, of course, reinforcement. Negative consequence can be as subtle as turning your back on the dog or as violent as squirting him with a jet of water.

For a clicker trained dog, self-correcting circumstances can be his negative consequence. Not getting the treat, being forced to end the game when wanting to continue, or having to look on while another dog plays the game, is often enough of a consequence to motivate the clicker trained dog to get back to work or to work harder.

Reinforcement for playing the game and negative consequence for not playing are functional elements in Clicker Training. The dog gains a perception of success and learns how to attain it rather than looking for ways to avoid physical correction. The ability to earn his own way by his own actions raises the dog's willingness and gives his trainer the chance of enjoying a high degree of training success.

DEALING WITH DISTRACTIONS

The local park could be a good place to introduce minor distractions, but a soccer game would be too much for a first time out. Start with minimal distractions in a controlled environment where other people and dogs are not likely to run up in an uncontrolled manner. Gradually increase distractions, always giving your dog a chance of being successful and earning reinforcement. Remember that distractions include smells on the ground. This is especially important to keep in mind when working on the thrown retrieve in new environments.

What seem to be subtle distractions to the trainer can turn into a huge distraction for the dog. If he's distracted stay close to him and raise reinforcement by doing one or more of the following:

✓ Bring out the best liver - the stuff you were saving in your pocket for just this occasion.

✓ Jackpot the dog for the smallest of compliance.

✓ Become very interesting by squealing, sitting down, or starting a game of tug or chase.

1 - 7 TARGETING

THE HYPE ABOUT TARGETING

From the time a puppy comes into this world he is targeting on something. Whether it is his mother's milk, his littermates' company, or the warmth from the heat lamp, he's targeting. When he comes to his food bowl, whenever he comes when called, when he goes out the door to do his "business," he is targeting.

Targeting behaviors are a main part of a dog's life and that makes them an important part of his training program. I play a fairly simple game of targeting with all dogs that come under my care, young and old. It can be played with puppies as young as 8 weeks, but most do better at 10 to 12 weeks of age. It's called the "Get It Game."

GET IT GAME

This game, although used to teach a dog to watch and then go to a target, also shapes:

✓ Reliable and fast recalls

✓ Fast and tight turns

✓ Beginner fronts

✓ Ignoring distractions

✓ Waiting for cues

With the dog on your left side, start by looping the leash into your left hand so you can easily let it out as the dog travels to the target. Place your fingers under the dog's collar – not on the leash, but in the collar. Have the treats in your right hand. At this point, the dog should not be required to sit – leave him standing.

I start this game in a kneeling position to not only be on the same level with the dog, but to gain better control over his actions. Say, "Mark!" and drop a treat just inches in front of him. He doesn't know what the command means at this time, but this is one of those few behaviors where the name goes on first.

Wait for the dog to see the target – with wriggly puppies this could take a little while and you might have to point to it. Do not release him until you feel him strain against the collar – this helps to build drive. Pause for just a second; don't wait too long or he'll lose interest and stop straining. Give him another new command, "Get it!" as you release the collar and the leash loops at the same time. Hold on the end of the leash; looping the handle over your wrist helps.

There is a valid reason for always having a leash on the dog. It eliminates the possibility of the dog becoming distracted from the game and finding reinforcement elsewhere. It is not to be used for collar corrections or to pull the dog back to you. Your dog knows with a leash on, he only has so much room to move. This heightens your ability to keep The Game moving FAST and to keep ALL the reinforcements under your control.

As soon as the dog gets to the treat, praise him! Do this a few times to get the idea that there will be good stuff out in front of you.

As you continue with the above steps, start to toss the treat a little ways and then farther, being careful not to exceed the length of the leash. As he becomes more proficient at that, and shows a lot of drive to get to the target, stand up and bend over. You are still holding the collar, looping the leash, and so on; that hasn't changed. You are just removing yourself from the game a little in not kneeling next to him anymore.

Here is the second phase to this game - the next step. It now becomes a "two-cookie" game where the dog gets the target treat and then is reinforced (click and treat) for coming when called.

When the dog's mouth is on the target treat, immediately give your recall command (dog's name, "Come!"). Since it is a dog's nature to look for a second treat any time he finds one, any head turn or ear flick in your direction might be where you start your reinforcement. CLICK for the very tiniest head turn in your direction, take a step or two backwards, move your right hand, which contains a second target, to the center of your body at the dog's nose level – somewhere around the knees for most dogs.

The primary reinforcement, the treat, should always come from center-front position, as this is where the dog will be expected to end up on all formal recalls. Being a picture-oriented animal, the more he sees this "picture" as the one where he is treated, the more he will strive to see it each time he is called. (We don't' need the sit in front at this time.)

The back up mentioned above is essential in shaping straight fronts for two reasons. The first is to "draw" him into a straight front position. Some of the targets are close, and long-bodied dogs will not have the opportunity to turn completely around and come in straight if you just stand there; you need to move out of his way. Muscle memory and the picture he sees when he receives the treat will remind him that it comes when his body is pointed straight at you. The second reason is to build drive. A dog that comes in fast and stays at a run until he reaches front position will not lose points for his speed in an obedience class.

Continue to work these steps, adding a mark signal if you plan to continue on to the AKC Utility class.

1 - 8 CLICKER TRAINING TERMS AND DEFINITIONS

Adduction – Combining two known behaviors into a new, and often undesirable, behavior.

AKC – American Kennel Club, the principal dog breed registry of the United States. For free information send a request to The American Kennel Club, 51 Madison Ave., New York, NY 10010.

Attention (from the trainer) – Paying attention to the dog in the form of eye contact or participating in the training game with him is a subtle reinforcement, and the removal of attention can be used as a subtle aversive.

Attention (from the dog) – The dog pays attention to the trainer or handler regardless of distractions; intense attention is required for obedience and conformation; periodic, or as-needed, attention is essential for herding and agility; loose attention is shaped for tracking.

Aversive – A punishment that causes the dog to abandon a behavior; conveys to the dog that a behavior is wrong and is to be avoided during the current shaping session.

Backward Chaining (back-chaining) – Teaching the last behavior of the chain first – chaining can take place in training within a single behavior, in which case, the backward chain would consist of teaching the last portion of a behavior first.

Behavior Chain – see Chain.

Behavior Marker – The conditioned reinforcer (clicker), that marks the desired behavior the moment it is offered.

Chain – A series of known behaviors performed in succession on one command.

Command-Based Training – Giving a dog verbal or signal commands followed by placing him in the desired position or physically causing him to perform the commanded behavior.

Conditioned Reinforcer – A behavior marker that tells the dog his behavior at the instant he hears it will earn him a primary reinforcement.

Conditioned Response – A learned behavior reliably offered on cue, never offered off cue.

Conditioned Stimulus – A learned signal (cue) that indicates when a certain behavior will be reinforced.

Consequence, negative – An aversive given when the dog fails to perform a known behavior or offers undesirable behavior(s).

Consequence, positive – Positive reinforcement.

Correction – See Aversive.

Criterion (criteria, *plural)* – The standard against which the dog's overall performance is judged by the trainer.

Crossover Dog – A dog that was a command-based subject and is now 100% clicker trained.

Crossover Trainer – A trainer who formerly used command based methods and is now using clicker training wherever possible.

Distraction – Anything that diverts the dog's attention away from his trainer or his work.

Don't Shoot The Dog! – An operant conditioning training guide written by Karen Pryor; considered by many to be the current "bible" of animal training.

Exhibitor – see "Handler"

Extinguishing a Behavior – When a known and reinforceable behavior fades and then dies out as a result of not being reinforced. .

Extinction Burst – An exaggerated version of a behavior before it is completely extinguished.

Fixed Schedule – One reinforcement per behavior or effort; used in initial shaping; produces little improvement.

Fluent, Fluency – Understanding a specific behavior or chain of behaviors from start to finish and performing it on command and under distracting conditions.

Handler – The person exhibiting a dog in breed, obedience, agility, tracking, coursing, or herding.

Imprint Training – Early learning that stamps information directly into the mind without deliberate external training.

Instructor – The person giving training advice and instructions to the trainer of the dog.

Jackpot – A larger than normal primary reinforcement that is given in one lump sum or several treats fed one at a time for several seconds.

Keep-going Signal (KGS) – A signal telling the dog that what he is doing will be reinforced but that he should continue doing it; useful for exercises in which the dog must work away from the trainer (hunting, herding, water retrieving).

Mouthing – When the dog rolls the dumbbell in this mouth, or chews on it while carrying.

Learning Dip – Momentary lapse during which the dog appears to have quit when in actuality he is just sorting it out in his mind.

Luring – Causing a behavior to be offered by enticing the action with treats or a toy.

Negative Punishment – Removal of something to decrease a behavior.

Negative Reinforcement – Removal of something to increase a behavior.

No Reinforcement Marker (NRM) – A signal that means no reinforcement is coming.

Off-Cue Behavior – When an animal offers a behavior for which no cue was given.

On-Cue Behavior – Behavior offered after its conditioned stimulus (cue) has been given.

Operant Conditioning – Reinforcing a behavior that is already occurring so that the dog will repeat it.

OTCh – The title added to the beginning of a dog's name after he earns an AKC Obedience Trial Championship.

Positive Punishment – Add a stimulus to decrease a behavior.

Positive Reinforcement – Adding something to the training game that will increase the probability that the behavior will occur again.

Primary Reinforcer – Whatever a dog will work to get.

R + – see "Positive Reinforcement."

Reinforcement – The process of clicking and treating the dog for offering a desired behavior or a series of desired behaviors.

Shaping – Deliberately reinforcing stronger responses and omitting reinforcement for weaker responses; allowing the dog to sort out what works and what doesn't.

Stimulus Control – Having a known behavior reliably executed on a conditioned stimulus (cue) 100% of the time. True stimulus control means: a) the behavior always occurs when the cue is given; b) the behavior is never offered if the cue isn't given; c) the behavior is never offered when a different cue is given; and d) no other behavior is offered in response to this behavior's cue.

Successive Approximation – Making each new behavior that is formed as a result of criteria increase as the only behavior that will be reinforced until the next raise in criteria.

Treat – The food or treat for which the dog will perform.

Trainer – The individual training the dog.

Training "W" – Two separate incidents that take place during the shaping process where the dog voluntarily, but temporarily, extinguishes known and reinforceable behavior.

Variable Quantities – Jackpots make training interesting for the subject and can build drive and intensify behavior.

Variable Schedule – Withholding reinforcement to intensify and/or increase reliability of an already shaped behavior.

SECTION 2

SHAPING
the RETRIEVE
ELEMENTS

AKC Obedience Retrieves
Understanding the Elements

2 - 1 RETRIEVE BASICS

The TAKE, GIVE, and FRONT behaviors have commands, their own stimulus control. Behaviors like the hold, carry, and turn, do not have separate commands, but are by-products of those that do. For the remainder of this section and in all of Section 3 of this book, behaviors with verbal commands – behaviors under stimulus control – are indicated by capitalization.

REQUIREMENTS

The Retrieve on the Flat and the Retrieve over High Jump are two of the required exercises in the AKC Open obedience class. The basic requirements for these retrieves are identical. The dog is required to:

- ✓ Remain waiting for the throw and the command to retrieve.
- ✓ Go briskly and directly to the dumbbell.
- ✓ Pick up the dumbbell without hesitation, mouthing, or dropping.
- ✓ Return directly to the handler.
- ✓ Perform a FRONT.
- ✓ Wait for the GIVE command.

Not performing the exercise by the above guidelines will cause a point loss for each offense or a zero (failure) for the exercise.

Constant Retrieve Components

All retrieves have six common components, whether performed in the field by a spaniel or in the obedience ring by a toy breed.

1. Wait for the command or signal (stimulus control).

2. Go swiftly to the object to be retrieved (the take).

3. Pick up the object (the take, the turn).

4. Return directly to the trainer with the object (the return, the hold).

5. Wait for the give command (the hold).

6. Give up the object willingly on command (the GIVE).

These six steps make up an obedience retrieve chain; they are the constants in that chain, the series of behaviors performed in a specific order, and executed on a single command. When the retrieve training is complete, the individual behaviors in the chain are general knowledge to the dog and can be use within or outside the chain. The chain may also be added to or subtracted from.

Variable Retrieve Components

1. Open and Utility obedience - remain at heel position before the retrieve, and then sit in FRONT after the retrieve.

2. Hunt tests - Deliver to heel position (optional).

3. Flyball – jump hurdles and trigger the mechanism that releases the object to retrieve.

4. Scent hurdles - Jump four hurdles then scent for the correct object to retrieve.

5. Service work – Pick up, carry and drop specified objects on command.

All common components are broken down into their smallest parts, which are the TAKE, hold, carry, and GIVE. Variable components such as STAYS, FRONTS, triggering a Flyball box, scenting, and jumping, are all shaped separately and added into each retrieve chain where appropriate. The TAKE, GIVE, and FRONT behaviors each have commands of their own and are each put on stimulus control before being built into the retrieve chain.

SCORING THE AKC OPEN CLASS

American Kennel Club (AKC) Obedience Regulations, Open Exercises and Scores, state the Open class exercises and maximum scores are:

1. Heel Free and Figure Eight .... 40 points

2. Drop on Recall .... 30 points

3. Retrieve on Flat .... 20 points

4. Retrieve over High Jump .... 30 points

5. Broad Jump.................................... 20 points

6. Long Sit.. 30 points

7. Long Down..................................... 30 points

Maximum Total Score .... 200 points

All dogs enter the ring with 200 points - a perfect score. For each mistake the dog or handler makes, the judge deducts from 1 to 5 points depending upon the severity of the mistake (for more information about scoring regulations, consult the AKC Obedience Regulations booklet). To pass an Open class, the dog must earn more than half of the available points for each exercise and end up with a minimum score of 170 points. After passing three times under three different judges, the dog earns the Companion Dog Excellent title and the letters "CDX" are suffixed onto his name.

Retrieve on the Flat Exercise Scoring

The retrieves make up 50 points of the entire points available in this class. Point deductions are as follows for the Retrieve on the Flat (paraphrased):

The dog will receive a score of zero (failure to pass) if he:

1. Fails to go out on the first command or signal

2. Goes out before the command or signal is given

3. Fails to retrieve

4. Does not return with the dumbbell sufficiently close to the handler that the dumbbell may be removed without the handler taking a step forward

5. The dog will receive a substantial point deduction (3 points or more) for

6. Slowness in going out or returning or in picking up the dumbbell

7. Not going directly to the dumbbell

8. Mouthing or playing with or dropping the dumbbell

9. Reluctance or refusal to release the dumbbell to the handler

10. The dog will receive a minor point deduction (2 points or less) for

11. Slow or poor sit (not prompt or smart)

12. Touching the handler with snout or dumbbell

13. Sitting between the handler's feet on the front

14. Not fronting   including going directly to heel position

Retrieve Over High Jump Exercise Scoring

The same deductions applied in the Retrieve on the Flat exercise apply to this exercise; those that concern the jumping portion of the exercise only are listed below.

The dog will receive a score of zero (he fails to pass) if he:

1. Fails to go over the full height of the jump, either going or returning

2. Climbs or uses the jump for aid in going over

3. The dog will receive minor to substantial point deductions, depending on the specific circumstances in each case for

4. Touching the jump in going over

5. Displaying any hesitation or reluctance to jumping

The only difference between the flat and the jumping retrieves is the presence of the jump. Although this book does not cover jumping, I have a word of advice regarding the subject.

The essence of the retrieve over high jump exercise is that the dog retrieves the dumbbell by traveling between two upright sticks (jump standards). As the jump is raised, the dog learns to continue to pass between the jump standards, but at a height that keeps him from running into the boards between them. For this reason, proofing should be performed with only one small board so your dog can concentrate on his path of travel alone. Once the correct path of travel is shaped beyond proofing, adding boards and teaching the jumping separately is recommended.

The Retrieve over High Jump chain contains more separate behaviors than any of the other AKC obedience class exercises. (The STAY, WAIT and FRONT are not taught as individual behaviors in this book, but are required behaviors for the execution of the obedience retrieve.)

ONE SIZE DOES NOT FIT ALL

An improperly fitted dumbbell can cause mouthing and dropping problems. Your investment of time and effort into measuring your dog and ordering a properly fitted dumbbell will payoff in large dividends if you plan to exhibit your dog in obedience.

You will need the following:

✓ Two wooden dumbbells made of lightweight wood and designed for your breed of dog.

    ✦ One dumbbell with a mouthpiece 1" longer than the measurement between the outside edges of the dog's upper canines. This is the training dumbbell.

    ✦ One dumbbell with a mouthpiece no more than 1/2" than the measurement between the outside edges of the dog's upper canines, unless it pinches the dog's lips. This is the working dumbbell. Mouthpieces that are much longer than described above are easily carried crooked and played with, so keep it as short as comfortably possible.

✓ If you are training a breed such as a Bloodhound the distance between the canine and the bell should be double so he doesn't bite his lips when picking up the dumbbell.

✓ All dumbbells should have bells wide (tall) enough that there is no danger of the dog scraping his chin or getting grass up his nose when picking it up.

✓ The bells should slant away from the dog's head, enabling him to see where he is going.

✓ Extra dumbbells of various weights as replacements for the first two, in case they get broken or lost (wooden dumbbells break if thrown on concrete and chip if thrown on asphalt).

✓ A short leash, for up close work; long, heavy leashes are distractions.

✓ A 6' leash for intermediate distances, again leather is preferred.

✓ A 16' or 26' Flex-i™ or a lightweight long line for distance work. Retractable leads make a clicking noise when the brake is applied. Mountain climbing ropes are nearly indestructible and come in many sizes, weights and pretty colors and patterns.

✓ Clicker or another unemotional, easily discerned behavior marker.

✓ Small, soft, and delectable dog treats.

TRAINER'S NOTE:

If you are planning to go on to Utility training with this dog, shape the TAKE up to the actual retrieve using a metal scent article.

When the dog is trained enough to perform thrown retrieves use a metal scent article for the occasional play retrieve.

Figure 1 – Holding the Dumbbell
Hold the dumbbell firmly in the right hand, taking care not to block the mouthpiece. No treats are in this hand.

2 - 3 RETRIEVE CHAINS

THE LINKS

The retrieve chain is made up of several totally separate behaviors that must be shaped separately then may be reinforced separately as the retrieve chain is being assembled. They are the wait (STAY), the send, the TAKE, the return (carry), the FRONT, and the GIVE (hold). Some behaviors -the TAKE, STAY, FRON T, and GIVE - must be brought under stimulus control before assembling the chain. When executed, all but the STAY and the GIVE are performed on one command.

These seemingly simple behaviors are made up of several parts, each of which must be shaped to perfection before the behavior is complete. Below are the separate parts listed in an order similar to the order in which they will be shaped. Each is a reinforceable behavior and each of these is dissected later in the workbook, during the actual shaping process.

Detailed Retrieve Components

The TAKE from Hand

- ✓ Look at the dumbbell
- ✓ Sniff the dumbbell
- ✓ Touch the dumbbell
- ✓ Nose, mouth, teeth, bite
- ✓ Reach to touch the dumbbell
- ✓ Take the dumbbell from hand
- ✓ TAKE from up, down, left, right
- ✓ Reach to TAKE the dumbbell
- ✓ Add the 'TAKE' cue
- ✓ Walk forward to TAKE the dumbbell

The Hold, Carry

- ✓ Head turn after a TAKE from hand
- ✓ First step after a TAKE from hand
- ✓ Turning carrying the dumbbell
- ✓ Taking the dumbbell from outstretched hand (distance added)
- ✓ Turning after the TAKE
- ✓ Walking after the TAKE
- ✓ Walking carrying the dumbbell
- ✓ Trotting carrying the dumbbell
- ✓ Fronting carrying the dumbbell

The TAKE from the Floor

- ✓ Taking from the floor
- ✓ Turning the head after the TAKE
- ✓ Looking up after the TAKE
- ✓ Taking a thrown dumbbell
- ✓ Turning the head after the TAKE
- ✓ Looking up after the TAKE
- ✓ Running to the dumbbell
- ✓ A good TAKE from a distance
- ✓ The tight turn after the TAKE

The GIVE (Hold)

- ✓ Releasing the dumbbell on command
- ✓ Holding the dumbbell in FRONT position

The front (Return)

- ✓ Running to handler carrying dumbbell
- ✓ Hitting FRONT carrying dumbbell

Proofing

- ✓ Put the chain together
- ✓ Click within the chain
- ✓ Add distractions
- ✓ Add a "judge" to call commands
- ✓ Retrieve past food

2 - 4 UNDERSTANDING THE RETRIEVE BEHAVIORS

This entire chapter explains the behaviors that the workbook will help you shape. The photographs in this chapter should be referred to while engaged in the shaping process.

To ensure that you understand all of the behaviors required in a good retrieve chain, how they are shaped, and how they are to be performed, please read this chapter and study the photographs before proceeding to the workbook where you will shape them.

THE TAKE

A reliable TAKE begins with reinforcement for looking at the dumbbell and progresses to biting, and then holding it. Through successive approximation, criteria are gradually added, resulting each time in a new behavior; each new behavior is closer to the TAKE behavior than its predecessor.

The TAKE grows from the look, the sniff, the touch, the bite and a few seconds of hold before it is a true TAKE behavior. All of its separate parts must be shaped before the trainer and dog can move on to retrieving.

Figure 2 – The Look
The TAKE behavior starts with a look or sniff. Being down on one knee gives two advantages 1) the trainer has a good view of what the dog is doing, and 2) working on the dog's level is less intimidating than bending over him.

Certain breeds are known to have high retrieve instincts. Dogs of these breeds often reach out and take the dumbbell from the trainer's hand at the first offering. When this happens the trainer, seeing no need to shape for behavior that is already occurring, might mistakenly skip over some of the prescribed shaping sessions.

The shaping of each part of the TAKE behavior is important to arrive at the desired result. Skipping ahead can cause problems later; lessons missed will represent voids in your dog's training program. For the dog that grabs without thinking, increase the criteria early by having him perform the TAKE while moving his head to the right or left and up or down. These easy additions will slow down the exuberant dog to a more useful thinking speed. When he is in a learning mode he is a "thinking" dog, and only then should you begin shaping the TAKE components.

There are "spoiled" dogs that will not lift a foot if they think they can be carried. These are the dogs that require the most patience for they will try to get the trainer to do both jobs; they are good people trainers. Reluctant or "slow" dogs, however, often make the best retrievers because their trainers are not able to bypass any steps in shaping the TAKE and hold behaviors.

If your dog should offer a behavior that surpasses the criteria for the first few shaping lessons, continue shaping the individual TAKE components, because there is a Training "W" in this dog's near future. If he is not allowed to experience it, he will not benefit from its lessons. If the Training "W" is not experienced during this early period in the shaping process, it will be more difficult to overcome when it does occur.

Shaping for a good TAKE is your insurance against holding and carrying problems in your finished dog. Make sure he is definite and confident in all aspects of the TAKE from your hand before progressing to a TAKE from the floor, from a thrown TAKE, and most certainly before FRONTing.

Shaping for the TAKE behavior should be done on the dog's level. I prefer to be on one knee, facing the dog's right shoulder with him sitting or standing, facing to my right. This puts little demand upon the dog to move his feet while getting his mouth to work. It also allows the trainer to be in the optimum position for preventing the dog from leaving and for caressing the dog after a good try.

Through successive approximation, the TAKE is shaped following an outline in the workbook section. The dog is first clicked for a look, then a sniff, a touch, a lick, a tooth touch, and a bite, until he can consistently TAKE and hold the dumbbell while it is still in the trainer's hand. He is ready for the cue to be added when he can walk forward to TAKE the dumbbell. The dumbbell is not released from the trainer's hand until the dog is ready to carry it while walking.

THE CARRY (HOLD)

Shaped in two separate parts, the hold has two representations - one is the carried hold and the other is the static hold. Each represents its own challenge to the dog. The following text explains how we get the hold as a result of shaping the carry. There is no need to shape the hold as a separate behavior or to put a name to it, since it cannot begin before executing the TAKE, and does not end until a GIVE command is issued.

The hold is the part of the retrieve that adds the mystery for some trainers; probably the result of trying to teach the dog to perform a static hold. Many trainers want to reinforce the hold rather than the TAKE by moving away from the TAKE too rapidly, before it is concrete in the dog's mind. Reinforcing the TAKE again and again reinforces the hold and gives it stability. There is no verbal command for the hold in this workbook since anytime the dumbbell is in the dog's mouth it *is* a hold and I see no reason to add a command for a behavior that is understood as just something that happens between the TAKE and the GIVE.

Until now the TAKE has been shaped from the dog's level, but to shape the carry, the trainer must be standing. To familiarize the dog with this new posture, we first have him perform several simple TAKES while holding the dumbbell. Dogs have a limited

Figure 3 – Turn and Carry
The hold is not taught separately, but as a part of the TAKE behavior. Here the dog is performing a turn after taking the dumbbell.

33

ability to generalize and a change in posture or position is like a change in background, so only change your posture, not your position with respect to the dog's position.

The head turn is an essential part of shaping for a reliable hold. It teaches the dog to immediately turn his head after performing a TAKE and to look for his trainer as he starts his return. The head turn then, through successive approximation over several shaping sessions, becomes the foundation for the carry and the carry becomes the hold. This entire shaping process works only because the hold is understood and is never addressed as a separate behavior.

If the dog is performing a good TAKE, you may change position so that the two of you are facing the same direction, putting the dog in an informal heel position. Hold the dumbbell behind your back until ready to ask for a TAKE, which is by this time on cue (from the workbook), and going nicely.

When shaping the TAKE your knees are kept straight while you swiftly bring the dumbbell around to a distance no farther than a few inches from the dog's muzzle. This causes your upper body to bend forward and over the dog somewhat. Quickly give the TAKE command. As the dog takes the dumbbell, remove your hand and stand straight. The dog will carry the dumbbell by turning his head. The intensity he gives it may or may not cause a foot movement for balance. His face will say, "Hey! You forgot something!" Click for this movement and do it quickly. Pick up the dropped dumbbell, feed your dog and congratulate yourself, because your dog has just executed his first hold and carry.

TAKE FROM THE FLOOR

Some dogs will just pick up from the floor with the first TAKE command while others need more shaping. For the latter, hold the dumbbell nearer and nearer the floor, clicking for each successful TAKE and ignoring any that didn't work out so well. This is continued until the dumbbell is flat on the floor. Getting it to the floor requires a few TAKES and once on the floor you will usually have to put one finger on it, then point to it for several TAKES, holding your finger farther away each time.

Figure 4 – Take from the Floor
The take from the floor or ground begins with a placed dumbbell. The dog learns to pick up, and then turn and carry without the trainer's hand in the picture.

For those dogs that spend days learning to pick up from the floor, be careful and observant, as you are now raising the criteria to a very high level. Taking the dumbbell from the owner's hand is a far different affair than picking it up from the floor, and long-term problems may arise here if pressure to perform is exerted.

When the dog can TAKE consistently from the floor you will start adding distance a step or so at a time, also working on the turn and the return while carrying the dumbbell. The FRONT isn't added yet.

Eventually working up to a 20' throw being careful not to get ahead of yourself or your dog is essential at this time. If he can't do a perfect TAKE, turn, and return from 2', he cannot do it from a longer distance. Work continues within the dog's capability while raising the distance criterion in small increments.

THE SITTING TAKE

This is not a behavior that would be performed in the obedience ring, but is an optional behavior, helpful for teaching the GIVE behavior and command.

All instances of clicking for a carry, which causes the dog to drop the dumbbell, have up until now occurred while the dog was facing the trainer. The reason for this is that dogs are picture-oriented animals. By reinforcing all holds while the dog is facing the trainer, we have already instilled one good retrieve habit in him – that dumbbell dropping takes place only while facing and being very near the trainer.

With the dog sitting in FRONT, you will present the dumbbell and give the TAKE command. Because dogs are also position-oriented animals and the TAKE was shaped with the dog standing, many dogs will stand up before taking. If this is the case with your dog, you will need merely to fine-tune the TAKE behavior to include taking while sitting. This is not difficult; just use all the skills you have gained up to this point and use the aversive of taking away the dumbbell by putting it quickly behind your back if the dog attempts to stand.

Further, since this is the relative position in which he has always been allowed and even encouraged to spit out the dumbbell, some additional time might be required to reinforce TAKING while sitting in FRONT position.

This seemingly minor change of position represents a <u>major</u> change for the dog.

PROOFING THE HOLD

> TRAINER'S NOTE:
>
> Be careful not to increase criteria in more than one area, an easy mistake to make when building your first chain. Analyze what your dog is telling you when he fails and look for areas where you might be adding too much new material.

For this behavior the dog must be able to FRONT while holding the dumbbell and to willingly accept the dumbbell while sitting in FRONT as discussed in the previous paragraphs. If the dog will not perform a TAKE from your hand while in FRONT, perhaps he will TAKE while in heel position and allow you to pivot in front of him.

Once the dog will readily hold the dumbbell while remaining in FRONT, you will begin proofing the hold by reaching forward to touch the dumbbell.

Since you have never before moved your hands while the dog was holding the dumbbell, and since dogs are picture-oriented animals, any hand movement will prompt most dogs to spit out the dumbbell. When the dog spits out the dumbbell

Figures 5a and 5b – Proofing the Hold
Shaping a good hold requires proofing of the hold by placing fingers on the dumbbell. Use the GIVE command when the dog doesn't move and start over if he does. Increase the intensity of the hold behavior by placing both hands on the dumbbell and lightly tugging.

because of your hand movement, you can issue a verbal aversive ("Icky"), pick up the dumbbell, and turn your back on the dog for a few seconds. Sometimes the dog will sit there as if to ask, "What'd I do?" but more often he will run around to front, enticing you to start the game again, to give him another try.

When you can move one hand without the dog spitting out the dumbbell, even if the movement is one finger moving one inch, mark it as a new behavior by clicking. Pick up the dumbbell before feeding to prevent the dog from restarting the game on his own. Click for each success, moving closer to the dumbbell with your hand until you can touch it first with one hand, then with the other, then with both hands at the same time while the dog remains motionless. My aversive for mouth movement is that my hand returns to my sides and then I start the move over again. To shape a firm hold you will eventually be able to push and pull on the bells of the dumbbell and click for a good, strong hold.

THE GIVE

TRAINER'S NOTE:

The GIVE cannot be shaped until the hold is secure. Do not attempt this until you can put both hands on the dumbbell without the dog trying to spit it out.

Clicker training etiquette calls for silence while shaping, so your dog should have heard little besides the TAKE or FRONT commands over the last three lessons. In fact, during the entire learning process from the look until now you should say little to the dog. This is to your advantage for shaping the GIVE, as you shall see.

The GIVE behavior is nothing more than a controlled spitting out of the dumbbell. The GIVE will come easily to the dog since he's been trying to do it ever since the first TAKE. Because the dog is conditioned to open his mouth at the sound of the click he will open it at the sound of your voice. With the dog sitting in FRONT holding the dumbbell and with both hands on the bells of the dumbbell, say your GIVE command and the dog will open his mouth.

Well, it's not totally as easy as that because when he opens his mouth the dumbbell does not fall to the floor as it has on every other occasion. By holding the dumbbell exactly where it was when you said the GIVE command, it is still in the dog's mouth even though his mouth is open. In order to get it out of his mouth, he must open wide and back his head off the dumbbell. If he gets up from the sit during this process, be gentle and quietly start the game over.

When the dog backs his head away after opening his mouth the GIVE takes on the look and feel of a clean and well-understood behavior.

FRONTING WHILE CARRYING

TRAINER'S NOTE:

If your dog does not know how to perform a FRONT, teach it separately. Shaping it while having the dog perform the hold and carry behaviors at this time could spell training disaster. Dogs that already know both the carry and the FRONT will require re-shaping of both to perform them simultaneously. Remember to lower criteria when adding new components.

Since the FRONT is the last behavior performed in the retrieve chain, and chains are taught in a backward sequence, it should already be a known behavior. You are merely adding the carry to the already known FRONT behavior, making it a retrieve FRONT.

36

The retrieve FRONT may be taught only after the dog is turning and carrying the dumbbell for some distance. You will shape it in separate sessions, but continue to work on the TAKE, turn, and carry until your dog is fluent at all three. Then, the previously shaped TAKE, turn, and carry behaviors and the steps for them may be repeated for teaching the FRONT.

With the dog standing in heel position, you take a step forward with one foot, reach out in front with the dumbbell, and give the TAKE command.

As the dog straightens from the turn, call him to FRONT position, but be ready for him to spit out the dumbbell, as commands have not been issued to him while carrying until now. If he does spit it out, stand still and look at the dumbbell. If he understands the FRONT, he will probably go to FRONT and wait for the treat, but will then remember the dumbbell and return to get it. This is all if you do not interfere, of course. This is a difficult time for trainers who want to help. You must resist the urge to help or show your dog how to do these behaviors. By being patient and allowing him to figure them out, you will strengthen all of these behaviors.

When the dog performs the FRONT while holding the dumbbell, click quickly - before he is all the way into the sit – before he begins mouthing the dumbbell. When he relaxes doing these fronts it's a sign that he's beginning to understand, and a time when you should delay the click for a second or two, creating a short hold. It is a good idea to wear hard shoes to protect your toes from the dropping dumbbell while shaping the FRONT.

When the dog can perform a retrieve FRONT from a short distance, repeat the carry lesson, but as the dog makes the turn, you take a few steps backward, and ask or wait for the FRONT. This adds three new components to the FRONT, which are actually the last components in the chain.

Never allow the dog to pick up a dropped dumbbell after he has been clicked for holding it unless he is executing a retrieve chain. The carry and FRONT is a mini-chain, but dropping at FRONT because of the click then being allowed to pick up the dumbbell and start over at this time, will teach the dog to play with and toss the dumbbell.

Figure 6 – Fronting while Carrying
Good eye contact and no mouthing are essential to a full-point front in the obedience ring. This picture shows a puppy that is still unsure of what all goes into the front, indicated by the dumbbell held in his molars and a front foot in the air.

TRAINER'S NOTE:

When the dog aborts the retrieve exercise and drops the dumbbell without having heard the click, allow him to return to get it as stated above.

However, the carry and FRONT together constitute a mini-chain, and dropping at FRONT and then being allowed to pick up the dumbbell and start over will teach the dog to play with and toss the dumbbell.

37

2 - 5 CHAINING

BEGINNING THE CHAIN

When you have shaped all the behaviors described earlier, you have the beginnings of a behavior chain. At this time your dog will be able to:

1. Leave your side to go to the dumbbell and pick it up.

2. Make the 180° turn and return to the handler.

3. Carry the dumbbell to FRONT position

4. Perform a sit while holding the dumbbell.

5. Hold the dumbbell until hearing the GIVE command.

It is now time to make all the known retrieve behaviors fit together like the pieces of a jigsaw puzzle, flowing smoothly from one to the next until the chain is fluent.

STRENGTHENING THE CHAIN

A chain is only as strong as its weakest link and a behavior chain is only as reliable as its least reinforced behaviors; chains have a way of falling apart if the innermost behaviors are not fluent to the dog. In order for a behavior chain to be fluent, the dog must be able to perfectly perform each behavior and know how it fits against those that come before and after it in the chain. He must also believe that each behavior has importance - we have taught him this by shaping each part of the retrieve as an individual behavior. The new chain may be enforced as a whole, but this leaves some of its individual behaviors subject to extinction. Click in the chain whenever the dog performs brilliantly. Fear of clicking within a chain, thereby temporarily breaking it, can create a sloppy or dysfunctional chain.

Clicking for individual behaviors can actually strengthen the chain. For example, if your dog just flies out as fast as he can to get the dumbbell, click that! Who cares if the dog spits out the dumbbell and runs back to get his treat? It was a great send and he needs to know it was a great send. Without that instant feedback the chain too quickly takes on its own personality and its imperfect components merge and then deteriorate all together.

TRAINER'S NOTE:

By randomly reinforcing the inner behaviors of a chain, you strengthen the chain as a whole and give the dog a fluency that will not diminish. You will see this fluency emerge when you click and your dog continues to perform the next behavior in the chain rather than aborting the entire chain to get the treat. The dog will at first perform only the behavior he is executing when clicked, but will soon continue to the next behavior, adding behaviors in the chain until he is completing the entire chain after being clicked. When your dog can do this he is truly fluent at the retrieve. Add distractions and proofing and you are ready for competition.

Now that you are in an actual chain, you want the dog to continue the chain by going back out and picking up the dumbbell anytime he has dropped it or failed to pick it up. Allowing a dog to restart or continue a broken chain whether it was broken by a click or by his own mistake, will furnish the glue of understanding that will hold the chain together for the dog's lifetime.

When all of the components are working perfectly you will be ready to add the wait at HEEL command. This is the last element to be added to the chain.

38

STIMULUS CONTROL – WAITING FOR THE COMMAND

The wait at heel position should be added only after all other components that make up the retrieve are crystal clear and the dog is performing them 100% of the time (except maybe the occasional crooked FRONT). The reasoning behind this is because there is a built-in correction to the wait component and without fluency in the rest of the chain, breakdowns can occur.

Start with your dog on a short leash and sitting in heel position if he knows the sit at heel – otherwise just allow him to stand and disregard further references to sitting. Hold onto his collar; give him your STAY/wait command, and toss the dumbbell a distance of 4' to 6' (do not throw farther than leash length because doing so will result in a leash correction). The dog will most likely struggle to go out for the TAKE; if he's sitting he will stand up, if he's standing, he might pull hard, sit, or lie down. Only send him when you are comfortable with his position, whether sitting, standing, or lying; I would personally never send a lying dog, but would wait for him to get up again, which he will. Regardless of his position, don't let go of the collar until he stops pulling.

When he stops pulling, let go and allow him to perform the retrieve. Not pulling has become a self-reinforcing behavior, as it is now reinforcement for not pulling. Continue the above until he offers a wait on his own, and then heavily reinforce each wait. Imagine his surprise and delight at that. Randomly reinforce good waits with either a click or a send.

When he can wait for each of five throws without getting up, release his collar, give your wait command, and then throw the dumbbell less than leash length. If he gets up before being sent, hold the leash so he can't get to the dumbbell (I give my verbal "Ack!" aversive here, but the mildest version, "Uhn-uhn"). Happily abort, get him back to you, have him SIT, and then send him again. There is no need to repeat the throw. If working from the stand, work the wait with the dog standing.

Figure 7 – Waiting for the Throw
The dog watches the dumbbell before and as it is thrown. It becomes his target when the send command is given.

Figure 8 – Waiting for the Send
When the dumbbell is thrown the dog follows it with his eyes, focusing on the spot until sent to retrieve it.

Until now we have pattern trained this dog with a throw then a send followed by another throw then a send. To put the retrieve on true stimulus control, throw the dumbbell then say the dog's name and a command other than the TAKE command. Be ready to reel him in the first couple of times until he starts listening to what you say rather than assuming you gave the TAKE command. He will begin to pay attention to *what* you are saying rather than reacting to any spoken word he hears.

For stimulus control on all obedience exercises I regularly mix up individual behaviors and entire exercises. Example: Throwing the dumbbell over the high jump then telling the dog to stand before going out in front of him for signal practice; scenting articles and then heeling away from the pile; heeling into a halt 20' from the scented article pile and then sending the dog to FIND it. Pattern-trained dogs used to be able to earn obedience titles with high scores, but that was before the addition of the new Open B and Utility B classes where the order of the exercises is mixed. The best way to earn high scores with an advanced dog these days is to enter the ring with a thinking dog rather than with one that is pattern-trained.

BEHAVIOR CHAIN PITFALLS

When a dog thinks of the FRONT as the only reinforceable behavior in the retrieve chain, the rest of the behaviors that make up the chain begin to deteriorate. Training a dog to the high level of understanding required to execute a perfect retrieve time after time requires two elements:

- ✓ The dog must be fully shaped in each of the separate behaviors (components) of the retrieve chain. Those that can be, should be under stimulus control.

- ✓ The dog must believe that each behavior in the chain is either being reinforced during the execution of the chain, or is about to be reinforced.

You already know that failure to shape each behavior to a level of reliability before building (embedding) it into the chain will develop an unreliable chain. What you might not know is that failure to reinforce those behaviors as the chain is being built can cause each behavior to become unreliable even though outside of the chain each is 100% reliable on cue. The lack of reinforcement within a chain is often due to the trainer's fear that once built, chains should not be taken apart.

This belief is one of the pitfalls of training the retrieve and is one of the most difficult for the trainer to understand, which is why I have addressed it more than once in this book. Clicking within the new chain while each behavior is still fresh and flexible helps to assure the dog that imbedded behaviors are still reinforceable, even after the chain is formed. Variable reinforcement of all behaviors in the chain will eventually cause each behavior in the finished chain to serve as reinforcement for the behavior it follows.

2 - 6 THE WORKBOOK

RETRIEVER COOKBOOK

The "cookbook" for training any and all dogs has yet to be written, since no two dogs learn alike and no two trainers train alike. These two factors alone make it nearly impossible to give infallible step-by-step instructions. Add to this the fact that the average dog owner doesn't have the time to devote that a full-time trainer has, and that he is at the mercy of the weather, since he probably doesn't have an indoor training facility.

The following pages will give the average dog owner and trainer tried and proven guidelines from which to work. The instructions are based on methods and sequences that have been successful with many trainers and dogs over a testing period of several years.

Imagine training a dog while sitting in a chair watching a rented movie. Watching television while training the TAKE portion of a retrieve prevents the trainer from putting excess pressure on the dog. I say this because of the many dogs I have seen fail to learn the TAKE because of a trainer who was trying too hard.

40

By having something else to do, the trainer allows the dog to learn and to make the choice of whether to perform. When it is entirely the dog's decision, he learns to train the trainer, another important function of clicker training. The food driven dog with a trainer who will allow him to work on his own can feasibly go from disinterest to performing a proper TAKE of the dumbbell in one training session.

WORKBOOK LESSONS

The following pages contain the very cookbook I earlier said couldn't be written. It's as accurate as a cake recipe that doesn't tell what temperature to heat the oven for baking the cake. The cook could still make the cake, having all the ingredients, but the final outcome will take experimentation with various oven temperatures.

This workbook is a guide only, and since I have not had the opportunity to train ALL dogs in the world, it is safe to say there are individuals who will train by the book and those who will not. I believe that most dogs won't have as many problems with the content of the lessons as they will have with impatient trainers. As with all training methods, the final outcome will take some experimenting on the part of the trainer, but most of all, to be successful with any training that takes thinking on the part of the dog, the trainer must allow the dog to think.

As you go through the workbook, perform the tasks as described, answer the questions, and follow the instructions for each answer. Be willing to repeat or backtrack in a lesson, giving your dog ample time to respond before doing the remedial work. If you allow response time and learning time your dog will progress.

The first part of the workbook contains steps to be taken for shaping each and every part of the TAKE behavior. The shaded blocks are trainer's notes. Read them for tips and reminders as you go through each lesson. There is a logical rising and lowering of criteria with every lesson; follow these closely to shape a reliable retrieve.

SECTION 3

THE RETRIEVE WORKBOOK

Retrieve Training Workbook
Shaping the Retrieve Elements

3 - 1 SHAPING THE 'TAKE' BEHAVIOR

The TAKE behavior is one of the most important in the retrieve behavior chain. Mouthing, dropping, and crooked carrying result in point deductions and constitute an unreliable retrieve.

Before your dog can perform a proper TAKE, he might need some dumbbell attention shaping. This preliminary shaping involves several components that precede the TAKE itself. They are:

- ✓ Look

- ✓ Static Touch

- ✓ Reach to touch

- ✓ Walk to touch

- ✓ Lick

- ✓ Open Mouth (Tooth) Touch

- ✓ Bite – up, down, left, and right

- ✓ Adding the Command

This is not to say that all dogs need shaping through these beginner steps. Some will perform a TAKE at their first glance of the dumbbell. These individuals, however, quickly extinguish the TAKE behavior when any rules for taking the dumbbell are enforced. Many dogs perform the first two components, the Look and the Touch readily enough when introduced to the dumbbell, but soon enter into the first dip of the Training"W" and require shaping through it.

Lessons 1 through 8 will walk you and your dog through shaping for the Look through the Bite behaviors. Watch for the dips of the Training "W", as they can be both entertaining and informative. More importantly, experiencing and triumphing over them will form a good foundation for future shaping attempts.

At the completion of this chapter the dog will be consistently approaching and biting down on the mouthpiece of a dumbbell while it is held in your hand. Keep this picture in mind, because the ability to bite and hold a dumbbell while it is being held is the cornerstone of a good hold.

Shaping a TAKE could last a few minutes or it could take a couple of weeks. If your dog requires weeks to get through these first lessons, give them to him – it's worth it. Early TAKE shaping is best done in side-front position, kneeling with the dog facing your right and you facing the dog's right shoulder (pseudo heel position) as indicated in Figures 2 and 9.

Have a short leash on the dog for teaching all parts of the retrieve up to the distance retrieve. The use of a leash minimizes the length of time that passes between each shaping lesson, and enables the trainer to better control the game.

Keep shaping sessions to a maximum of ten minutes with no pressure, and five minutes with pressure on the dog. If you are the type of person who must remind herself not to "get in the dog's face" and demand results, keep it short. Ten minutes is acceptable for a patient trainer and a willing dog. If you don't feel you are done with your lessons and you feel that the dog can easily tolerate more, take a short break and then begin a new shaping session.

Refer to Figure 2 for positioning in Lessons 1 through 9. Here I am working at the dog's level rather than bending over her. This lowered position allows me to remain on his right side (heel position), to better control his actions, and to better observe his responses. Side benefits to this lowered position are that I am able to pet, talk in a low and soothing voice, and reinforce quickly.

The following lessons are written in a step-by-step format, each containing instructions on what to do next. As you perform each task, answer the question, and then proceed to the step number designated by your answer. Unless instructed to quit or proceed, drop down to the next step and follow the instructions found there. If your instruction is to quit a lesson, any steps following it are to be ignored.

GET THE LOOK – LESSON 1

TRAINER'S NOTE:

Lessons 1 through 9 are to be performed with the dog under physical control. It is important to hold the dog by the collar rather than telling him to STAY if he won't stay with you and work these lessons.

The "look" is addressed here because dogs are good at just staring at a trainer or a treat until both are his. If your dog will not look at a dumbbell in the presence of food or to get a treat, he will most likely not be a reliable retriever. Work this lesson – it's important.

The 1", 2", and 4" distances that follow in these lessons are for an average sized dog. Adjust them according to the size of the dog you are training. Giant breeds will require more distance, while toys will require less.

While kneeling or sitting in a chair and with the dog on your left or at side front (see Figure 2) -

1. Hold the dumbbell in your right hand in front of the dog's muzzle, no more than 1" away. Be certain you are holding it by the bell and that your hand is otherwise empty. Be silent and allow the dog to work – he will discover on his own how to get paid if you are just being supportive.

2. Reinforce (R+) for any obvious look or head movement toward the dumbbell, regardless of how slight or brief. Remain at this level resisting the desire to go ahead too quickly; the look, sniff, or lick at this time is out of curiosity and doesn't necessarily represent any understanding.

3. Is the dog showing a willingness to look at or move his head toward the dumbbell?

    a. YES - go to #4.

    b. NO - go to #8.

4. Work for <u>five</u> more looks.

5. Delay R+ for a few seconds after the next look.

6. Did he sniff or otherwise touch the dumbbell?

    a. YES – go to #7.

    b. NO – go to #8.

7.   Quit or proceed to the next lesson.

8.   Have you been working on this lesson for more than 10 minutes?

   a.   YES – go to #9.

   b.   NO – go to #10.

9.   Quit and repeat this section at your next scheduled shaping session.

10.   Rub a good smell on the dumbbell mouthpiece and repeat this lesson from #1.

TOUCH – LESSON 2

TRAINER'S NOTE:

Start out giving reinforcement (R+) for any touch by the muzzle, nose or chin, on any part of the dumbbell. Quickly raise criteria to R+ for a touch by the nose only, and then on the mouthpiece only, by not clicking for other behaviors and clicking for those you want. Be ready for a learning dip here and stay the course.

Your dog discovers during this lesson that your other hand holds the clicker and maybe the treats. You will need to hide that hand behind your back or in your armpit repeatedly until the dog stops going for it. I prefer the cookies in my mouth or in a bowl that is slightly out of reach to the dog.

After each touch, the dumbbell should be removed from the picture and then repositioned for the next touch. I place it under my left arm before treating the dog. I recommend you do it, too. If you make a mistake and present the clicker instead of the dumbbell, or click the clicker at the wrong time, just laugh it off and treat the dog. You are learning, too, and your dog is a forgiving creature.

1.   Hold the dumbbell in your right hand in front of the dog's muzzle, no more than 1" away. Be certain you are holding it by the bell and that your hand is otherwise empty.

2.   R+ the first four looks or head movements in the direction of the dumbbell to cover old ground.

3.   Delay the R+ after the four looks or head movements.

4.   Are you seeing a willingness to reach out and touch the dumbbell?

   a.   YES – go to #5.

   b.   NO – go to #7.

5.   Work until you can R+ for the touch four times.

6.   Quit or proceed to the next lesson.

7.   Have you been working for more than 10 minutes?

   a.   YES – go to #8.

   b.   NO – go to #9.

8.   Quit for now, but repeat this lesson until the #4's answer is YES.

9.   Rub something good smelling on the mouthpiece and repeat all steps from #1.

REACH TO TOUCH – LESSON 3

> TRAINER'S NOTE:
>
> If the dog has not yet offered to touch the dumbbell without having to reach for it, master Lesson 2 before moving on to this lesson.

1. Start this lesson with the dumbbell no more than 1" from the dog's muzzle.

2. R+ for four touches, again, covering old ground.

3. Move the dumbbell so it is now 2" away from the dog's muzzle but still directly in front of it.

4. Is the dog showing a willingness to stretch his neck and reach to touch the dumbbell?

    a. YES – go to #4.

    b. NO – go to #7.

5. Is the dog consistently stretching to touch the dumbbell?

    a. YES – go to #5.

    b. NO – go to #8.

6. R+ the reach to touch four times.

7. Quit or proceed to the next lesson.

8. Return to Lesson 2 and work until the dog will offer two touches for one R+, and then return to #1 of this lesson.

9. Reduce the distance of the dumbbell, R+ for several touches, and then increase the distance again.

10. Did this work?

    a. YES – go to #4.

    b. NO – go to #7.

WALK TO TOUCH – LESSON 4

> TRAINER'S NOTE:
>
> It's important to keep this a low-key exercise, with no pressure placed on the dog, but very much under your control; do not insist on a sit or stand.
>
> Hold your hand in a static position while waiting for the touch behavior; this is not a moving target at this time. Do not "lure" the dog with the dumbbell or move it toward his snout; to do so at this time is setting your dog up for failure, telling him you are not to be trusted.

1. Start out holding the dumbbell 4" from the dog's muzzle.

2. Does the dog readily stretch his neck and reach out to touch the dumbbell?

    a. YES – go to #2.

    b. NO – go to #4.

46

3. Move the dumbbell far enough away that it is difficult to reach by just stretching his neck.

4. Is the dog offering to take a step forward to touch the dumbbell? Or, if he is sitting, is he attempting to stand?

   a. YES – go to #8.

   b. NO – go to #5.

5. Move the dumbbell closer (lowering criteria), and R+ for a few touches then repeat from #1.

6. R+ his movement four times.

7. Repeat Lesson 3 to build drive, and then return to this lesson

8. Quit or proceed to the next lesson.

Figure 9 – Walk Forward to Touch
This picture demonstrates several key points. After getting a good reach to touch in the previous lesson, hold the dumbbell far enough away that the dog must walk forward a step or two to touch it. Notice that the trainer is working at side-front position, giving the dog a view that doesn't include the trainer. This puppy is already offering an open mouth touch.

LICK – LESSON 5

TRAINER'S NOTE:

Hold the dumbbell steady, taking care not to push it toward the dog's mouth at any time; he must make the decision to place a part of his mouth on the dumbbell.

This is a major increase in criteria, meaning that other criteria must be relaxed. R+ for any open mouth touches on any part of the dumbbell. You can always raise it again later to exclude the bells.

Most dogs never lick the dumbbell, but go right on to trying to bite it. Licking is what nervous dogs offer. If you have a nervous dog, work this lesson in its entirety.

If your dog begins this lesson with an open mouth touch, proceed to Lesson 6.

1. Hold the dumbbell in the right hand no more than 2" from the dog's muzzle.

2. R+ for <u>four</u> touches.

3. Withhold R+ after the <u>fourth</u> touch, if all touches have been immediate. Otherwise, work several more touches, delaying the click for just a split second to try to build up the dog's drive.

4. Is the dog showing a willingness to lick, or to the dumbbell when R+ is delayed or withheld?

    a. YES – go to #5.

    b. NO – go to #7.

5. Repeat for five licks or other open-mouth touches.

6. Quit or proceed to the next lesson.

7. Work this lesson until the dog is showing interest in opening his mouth in the direction of the dumbbell then repeat the entire lesson.

TRAINER'S NOTE:

From this point forward, be ready for the Training "W." Your dog will be doing well, exhibiting excellence in a lesson and then stop working. He might look at you, offer other behaviors, bite at the clicker, paw at the clicker or dumbbell, or all of these behaviors.

This is the first learning dip in the Training "W." Patiently work through it by waiting. Don't talk, move, or help other than to lower criteria if you feel it's necessary. The worst thing you can do is to move the dumbbell around like a toy and try to entice him.

He will return to the desired behavior, but be ready for the second learning dip. Treat it the same; on the other side of this dip is true success.

OPEN MOUTH TOUCH – LESSON 6

> **TRAINER'S NOTE:**
>
> Late clicking (R+) causes shaping problems. R+ as soon as the dog opens his mouth even if he is not yet touching the dumbbell. Giving R+ when you see the touch could be too late; the dog's thoughts may have already moved on. You will have the opportunity to delay the clicker later.
>
> Keep a good hold on the dumbbell in this exercise. Avoid dropping it and do not let your dog have it if he bites hard and tries to take it – it is a bite lesson, not a take lesson.
>
> The dog might chatter his teeth as he touches. This is a normal reaction, particularly if the dumbbell is a metal scent article.

In this lesson, begin holding the dumbbell out of sight. Present it to the dog and give him the opportunity to touch, lick, or bite it. Presenting the dumbbell to him "out of the blue," is an important step to teaching the dog to wait and watch. It also gives a crisp start for the game.

1. Have the dumbbell out of sight - behind your right leg is a good place - then bring it out and hold it no more than 2" from the dog's muzzle.

2. R+ the first <u>four</u> licks the dog offers. He might become excited over this new development of having the dumbbell appear and disappear. He might go looking for it. Don't let him shape you into giving it to him by this behavior, but patiently lure him back into position with a treat and start over. He will quickly learn that the game starts only when he is patient.

3. Withhold R+ on the next couple of touches, watching for a learning dip. (Learning dips may be displayed by the dog's pawing at the dumbbell, walking around, or whining...just wait.)

4. Did the dog touch the dumbbell with his teeth?

    a.   YES – go to #5.

    b.   NO – go to #8.

5. Delay R+ until the dog will place his mouth ON the mouthpiece of the dumbbell for an instant.

6. Jackpot the dog.

7. Quit or proceed to the next lesson.

8. Repeat Lesson 5 to build drive before returning to this lesson. Repeat this Lesson from #1.

TRAINER'S NOTE:

Allow the dog's mouth to come to the dumbbell. Refrain from pushing it toward him or waving it around in front of his face.

R+ as soon as the dog's mouth is over the mouthpiece. Do not hesitate. Late clicking presents problems, while early clicking builds drive.

This is where the dog starts to TAKE the dumbbell in his mouth trying to carry it. Hold on tight and click him for a good bite (a good hold). Do NOT let him take the dumbbell from your hand at this time.

Remain encouraged if your dog is touching with open mouth but NOT holding. It will come later.

1. Have the dumbbell out of sight (behind your right leg) then bring it out and hold it no more than 2" from the dog's muzzle.

2. R+ the first <u>four</u> open-mouth touches the dog offers, putting the dumbbell out of sight after each R+ then presenting it again for a new bite.

3. Delay R+ until the dog places his canines over the mouthpiece. He might remove his mouth before you click – just wait for him to repeat the behavior and click immediately.

4. Did the dog open his mouth and in any way bite the dumbbell?

    a. YES – go to #5.

    b. NO – go to #7.

5. Withhold R+ for soft bites, R+ only strong bites and attempted TAKEs. Repeat for <u>five</u> hard bites or attempts to TAKE.

6. If possible, delay R+ until the dog holds the dumbbell for a few seconds. Don't let go – you have to hold it, too.

    a. Repeat <u>four</u> times. Not all dogs will hold at this point, so if he doesn't, don't worry – he will soon.

7. Quit or proceed to the next lesson.

8. If the dog does not want to close his mouth on the dumbbell, try taking it away while his mouth is on it, and then representing it to him. Losing the thing that gets him R+ might be enough to make him bite it.

9. If possible, delay R+ until the dog holds the dumbbell for a few seconds. Don't let go – you have to hold it, too.

    a. Repeat <u>four</u> times. Not all dogs will hold at this point, so if he doesn't, don't worry – he will soon.

10. Return to Lesson 6 and work into this lesson for your next training session.

> Remember as always, to allow the dog's mouth to come to the dumbbell. Refrain from pushing it toward him or waving it in front of his face.
>
> R+ as soon as the dog's mouth is over the mouthpiece. Do not hesitate.
>
> The dog may want to TAKE the dumbbell in his mouth, trying to carry it, but don't let go. Hold on tight and click him for a good bite (a good hold).

Have the dumbbell out of sight (behind your right leg) then bring it out and hold it within 4" to 6" of the dog's muzzle.

1. R+ the first <u>four</u> bites the dog offers, putting the dumbbell out of sight then bringing it back out for each touch. Remember to hold onto the dumbbell.

2. Raise the dumbbell high enough that he must reach up to get it, and low enough that the bell touches the floor. Hold it far enough to the right and to the left that he must reach for it, picking up one foot to do it.

3. Did the dog readily open his mouth and bite the dumbbell whether it was high or low, left or right?

    a. YES – go to #4.

    b. NO – go to #6.

4. Repeat from Step #2 <u>four</u> times.

5. Quit and read the information at the bottom of this lesson page.

6. Return to Lesson 7 and work it again. Make sure all your answers are "YES" before returning to this lesson.

NOTE: The following lesson adds the command to the TAKE behavior. Do NOT proceed unless you are confident that your dog has mastered all tasks in the previous eight lessons.

ADDING THE COMMAND – LESSON 9

The verbal cue or command is given prior to the presentation of the dumbbell. You want your dog to be quick at the sound of the command to TAKE, so you want to be quick about presenting the dumbbell after giving the command.

You will still be holding onto the dumbbell throughout this section. Don't let him take it from your hand, yet. That comes when he is ready to carry it – when you add the turn.

Clicking early here will be of benefit to your dog - more importantly, don't click late.

1.   Have the dumbbell out of sight (behind your right leg).

2.   Swiftly bring the dumbbell out from its hiding place to within 4" to 6" inches of the dog's muzzle.

3.   Just as the dumbbell reaches the point at which you will stop its motion, give your TAKE command ("Fetch it," "Take it," "Get it)".

4.   Keep holding the dumbbell and R+ as soon as the dog attempts to bite or TAKE it.

5.   R+ the TAKE even if the dog has in the past been carrying objects such as toys. You are reinforcing the TAKE on command, not the carry.

6.   Add criteria by holding the dumbbell farther away, up, down, and to the right and left, giving the command just before the dumbbell is in position.

7.   Further increase criteria by holding the dumbbell up to 12" from the dog so he must also walk toward it.

3 - 2 TURNING, HOLDING, CARRYING

SHAPING A GOOD HOLD – LESSON 10

In this lesson there is nothing for the reader to do but to read this text. The retrieve hold is one of the great mystery areas for far too many trainers. To be successful at teaching your dog a reliable hold, keep in mind that dogs don't retrieve toys or rabbits, and then sit quietly with them in their mouths. To do so would be unnatural behavior, yet this is the very behavior most trainers begin with when training for the retrieve.

While engaged in shaping the following lessons, consider the hold as behavior that occurs between the TAKE and the GIVE commands. By shaping a TAKE and simply encouraging the dog to carry the dumbbell, the hold behavior is being performed; it is being shaped. The hold should be all but

Figure 10 – Small Step Forward
By taking a small step forward and letting go when the dog takes the dumbbell, a turn is created along with a short carry and a hold.

ignored by the trainer, as it is a by-product of both the TAKE and the carry behaviors, and is not regarded as a separate behavior until shaping the GIVE command. While teaching the

52

GIVE, the hold is proofed, but again is not shaped as a separate behavior, and is not given a command of its own.

The following method has worked with many dogs, but is dependent upon the trainer working each lesson until the dog is fluent in that behavior. Moving ahead with a dog that is not ready is sure to cause problems and insecurities later on, so hang in there and work the dips and enjoy the successes as they come.

Hold and carry shaping begin with the turn, which also teaches a tight turn and fast return to the trainer.

GETTING A TIGHT TURN – LESSON 11

TRAINER'S NOTE:

It is expected that the dog will spit out the dumbbell when clicked, regardless of whatever else he is doing after the TAKE. Never admonishing him for it will build fluency in the chain and in the hold – honest.

Any time the dog begins mouthing the dumbbell you are getting a signal that you are moving ahead too fast or clicking too late, or both.

Until now you have been working on the dog's level. It is time to stand up and face in the same direction as your dog. Do so with the awareness that your change in posture constitutes a rise in criteria. This rise in criteria may require you to back track for a minute or two of remedial TAKE shaping.

1. With your dog sitting or standing at heel position, and with the dumbbell out of sight, perform the following steps:

2. Bend over slightly as you swiftly reach in front of the dog with the dumbbell about 6" in front of his muzzle. Do not move your feet.

3. Give your TAKE command.

4. As the dog reaches out and bites the mouthpiece, release your grip and stand up straight. This causes you to look as though you have backed away from the dog even though your feet didn't move. Because you have always been in the previous TAKE pictures, he will wonder where you are and turn to look in your direction.

5. R+ as soon as you straighten up. His face will be saying, "Hey, you forgot this thing!" You are clicking for this brief hold; waiting to see the head turn before you R+ will be far too late.

6. Repeat the head turn only a few times before moving on or mouthing will result. Do not withhold clicking for any reason during this lesson.

TRAINER'S NOTE:

The click will cause the dog to immediately spit out the dumbbell. YOU must pick it up before feeding him the treat. It is important that YOU and not your dog restart the game.

Giving commands to SIT or STAY equal raising criteria and should not be used at this time. Commands other that the TAKE right are nothing more than distractions.

THE DOG'S FIRST CARRY – LESSON 12

1. Step forward one <u>small</u> step with your dog at heel position – Figure 10.

2. If your dog does not understand the stay or if he won't stay in this game, just hold him by the collar.

3. Hold the dumbbell out in front of the dog and at arm's length. For long-bodied dogs, this could be a reach. For toy breeds it can be done on a table.

Figure 11 – A Short Hold, Turn, and Carry
Until now the dumbbell has been held through each take behavior. By letting go you can obtain a short hold and carry. This puppy is holding nicely and making the turn to come back to the trainer.

4. Give your command to TAKE the dumbbell. If you are holding the collar, release it the instant you give the command.

5. Release the dumbbell as soon as the dog has taken the first bite.

6. R+ the dog for following you even if it is just with his head as shown with the puppy in Figure 11.

7. Be sure to click before he realizes he is carrying a dumbbell and starts to mouth it. The first sign of mouthing is a head drop. If this happens, simply abort the exercise, release the dog, and begin again, this time clicking sooner, before the dog can fail in either thought or action.

TURNING AND CARRYING – LESSON 13

TRAINER'S NOTE:

There is a chase game involved in shaping the turn and carry, which takes the dog's mind off the dumbbell in his mouth. It is very important to keep the chase short. Any more than just a few steps and the dog will mouth or drop the dumbbell, giving you nothing to R+.

Begin this lesson with the dog at heel position; again, no commands. If he won't stay on his own, hold him by the collar.

1. Take a step forward with your right foot as in Figure 10. Swiftly reach in front of the dog with the dumbbell at a distance from 6" to arm's length in front of his muzzle. You will be bent over.

2. Give your TAKE command, let go of the dog, and as soon as he bites the mouthpiece let go of the dumbbell, and straighten up as in the previous lesson.

3. Add criteria by quickly taking a step or two backward. This is a rise in the distance criterion.

4. R+ as soon as he completes the turn and starts to straighten out. If you wait until he gets all the way to you to R+ it will be too late. He could already be mouthing or thinking of dropping the dumbbell.

54

5. If the dog mouths during his return to you, you might be clicking too late.

6. If the dog mouths during his return to you, the distance might be too far for him at this time, so take only one step back.

7. As you repeat this lesson, watch for the dog to begin tightening his turn. He'll tighten it when he understands there is a bit of chase to this game.

8. Repeat this lesson several times before quitting and watch as he becomes better and better at it.

THE RETURN, ADDING DISTANCE – LESSON 14

TRAINER'S NOTE:

In this section your dog will learn to consistently execute a tight turn and a fast return to you. It is now a mini-chain that can be taken apart and put back together.

Cover old ground by taking a small step forward and getting a small turn as in Lesson 12, then work Lesson 13 a few times before proceeding.

Calling the dog to you is an optional later in this lesson, but will cause most dogs to drop the dumbbell. He is waiting for the click, so any sound – such as your voice – will distract him and serve as a click.

1. This lesson begins with a raise of criteria in more than one category, so be willing to lower criteria elsewhere, like holding his collar if he doesn't want to wait patiently.

2. Work as before. This time, however, when you step forward, make it a giant step and reach way out in front with the dumbbell – Figure 12.

3. Work #1 until your dog can handle the giant step before proceeding to another criteria increase in the next step.

Figure 12 – Take a Giant Step
The giant step increases the distance and gives the dog the opportunity to make the turn and get back to FRONT position.

4. Work as above, taking the giant step forward, but this time when you take back your step, also take two or three quick steps backward.

5. R+ him when he is straight and traveling toward you.

6. If he drops the dumbbell, pick it up, look sad and say you're sorry but that wasn't what you wanted, and start over.

Figure 13 – Take Back the Step
Take back the giant step and draw the dog to you. Giving a front command may be used but might be a distraction.

7. Continue these steps until he is solid. Quit here if he is tired or shows any boredom and resume from the beginning of this lesson at your next shaping session.

8. When clicking within this mini-chain, your dog will spit out the dumbbell every time he hears the click. YOU pick it up and give him the treat. Do NOT allow him to pick up the dumbbell at this time.

9. Click various portions of the turn and return, as they become faster, tighter, and straighter, while ignoring or aborting less than adequate performance. By alternating between clicking the turn and the return, they are both being placed on a variable schedule.

BREAKING THE MINI-CHAIN – LESSON 15

TRAINER'S NOTE:

You can now R+ anywhere in this chain; as soon as he begins his turn or when he grabs the dumbbell. You are breaking down the soon-to-be retrieve chain before it is fully formed, clicking for good behaviors that exist within it.

1. Start varying the retrieve by calling and not calling the dog to FRONT and by taking a variable number of steps backward. Keep in mind that at any time he could anticipate a previous R+ and spit out the dumbbell.

2. Now that we have added distance, allow the dog to pick it back up if he gets confused and drops it. Vary clicking for picking it back up (restarting of the retrieve game) or for any of the following:

3. Picking up then looking into your face.

4. Picking up then taking a few steps toward you.

5. Picking up and quickly finding front position.

6. Continue clicking each component in the retrieve chain. Maintaining each behavior as a separate and reinforceable behavior will enhance the performance of each component, which will enhance the chain.

Figure 14 – The Front
Shape the front behavior separately and add it to the chain when the dog will return to you while carrying the dumbbell.

7. Give your dog a reason to reinitiate the game (and speed up his return) by tossing a treat between your legs as he gets close to FRONT position. He is expected to drop the dumbbell to get the treat. Allow him to do this, and just wait for him to resume the retrieve. Click as soon as he picks up the dumbbell. Pick up the dropped dumbbell before feeding the treat.

8. The more you do step #4, intermingled with fronts, you will see him not only pick up, but also proceed to front position.

9. You may begin giving a gentle aversive like turning your back if he drops the dumbbell while returning. Add distractions that could cause this to happen; it will get him ready for distractions he'll encounter in the ring.

10. Turn back around or wait while facing the other way for him to resume the return *with* the dumbbell if he spits it out on the return. I normally like to turn back around and wait and watch, trying not to smile or giggle, being silently supportive and sympathetic

3 - 3 WORKING THE RETRIEVE CHAIN

MAINTAINING THE GAME – LESSON 16

The retrieve, particularly when a jump has been added, is a chain that requires shaping of all its elements until it is completely fluid, regardless of distractions and conditions. Even after it is fluent, maintenance is a must.

To encourage the dog to run out, TAKE, turn, and run back without consciously thinking about holding or carrying the dumbbell, requires the use of variable reinforcement.

Increase speed during the TAKE -from-hand shaping by ignoring slow responses or by snatching the dumbbell back if he is just walking to it. Trot off with it a few steps, saying something like, "Uh oh! It's mine and you can't have it". This game will increase his drive to get the dumbbell before the trainer changes his mind.

The dog will always view the retrieve behavior as a wonderful game if it is presented and then maintained as such. Working with short games and using of bits and pieces of the retrieve will keep it new and exciting for the dog. It's when trainers become serious that dogs also become serious, and then they become worried. Worry leads to mistakes, fear of being wrong, and a failure to work. Keeping it light can prevent stress from entering into your retrieve.

As your dog becomes more reliable at performing the retrieve chain, click during the chain. Click if he turns really fast, if he starts the turn before he's even done picking up, and for maintaining his speed beyond a point where he previously slowed down. Click when he gets up faster from the sit, and when he sits fast in FRONT position. Yes, he'll probably spit out the dumbbell, but that's okay. After he gets his treat, just stand there and wait. You'll see his little brain working as he realizes he's with you and neither of you have possession of the dumbbell. Click him for returning to it.

Eventually you will be able to click everywhere and anywhere in the chain and he'll just finish the chain. When this is accomplished the dog is truly fluent at the retrieve. When he can continue after a click with new surroundings and new distractions, he's ready for the obedience ring.

TAKE FROM THE FLOOR – LESSON 17

TRAINER'S NOTE:
It is still expected behavior for the dog to spit out the dumbbell at the sound of the clicker.
Try not to bore the dog.
Always end a shaping session with him wanting to do more.

As in the previous lessons, hide the dumbbell until you are ready to give your TAKE command. You may use small or giant steps in this lesson, depending upon how well your dog does. If he can't handle a giant step, take a small step instead. Do not take steps backward in this lesson.

1. Cover some old information and present the dumbbell to the dog for a few simple TAKES from the hand, reinforcing only those that you like and ignoring those you don't, before proceeding with this lesson.

2. Hold the dumbbell so that one edge of the bell is touching the floor directly in front of the dog.

3. Give your TAKE command.

4. R+ as soon as the dog's mouth is on the dumbbell. Watch for a slight head turn, as the dumbbell is no longer parallel to the floor.

5. Since this is a raise in criteria, hold on to the dumbbell, which is lowering hold and carry criteria.

6. Repeat these steps until the dog shows no hesitation in biting the dumbbell even though it is touching the floor.

7. Now, place the dumbbell on the floor and touch it with one finger.

8. Work as above, clicking him for biting it. Allow him to pick it up and stay aware that it will drop at the sound of the click. Pick it up; do NOT let the dog pick it up.

9. Place the dumbbell on the floor and have your hand near but not touching it and work as in #8.

10. Continuing placing the dumbbell on the floor and clicking him for picking it up until he can do it without you bending over.

TAKE FROM THE FLOOR, ADDING DISTANCE – LESSON 18

TRAINER'S NOTE:

Be careful not to go too fast here. This is an area where life-long habits are developed.

Here's a word about anticipation: Performing a behavior before it is asked for, is generally thought of as a bad thing. It is – in the obedience ring. In the shaping process, however, anticipation is a very good thing.

Anticipation teaches the dog:

✓ That anticipating a command or reinforcement reaps no benefit.

✓ Holding the dumbbell until he is clicked is reinforceable behavior.

✓ That all or none of the separate parts of the retrieve behavior might receive R+ at any time and not to expect R+.

Figure 15 – First Take from the Floor
By placing the dumbbell on the floor about two feet in front of the dog, you add distance. Until recently your hand has been a part of the behavior, so takes without it raise criteria.

58

1. With the dog standing or sitting in heel position, take a giant step forward and place the dumbbell on the floor 2' to 3' away.

2. Do not tell the dog to stay; stays are added last in the chain, after the rest of the retrieve chain has been built. Work on STAYS separately.

3. Send the dog to perform the retrieve with your TAKE command.

4. R+ the instant he picks up. I realize it's difficult to refrain from doing full retrieves, but just R+ the TAKE for now.

5. Repeat #1 through #4 <u>four</u> times before moving on, or until he shows no hesitation at moving forward and biting the dumbbell.

6. Raise the criteria with a delay of R+ on the next pick up. He will most likely spit out before you click, since he has a little built-in timer. If he does, he is just anticipating the click. Wait...do not interfere!

7. When the dog picks up the dumbbell to resume the retrieve, R+ the instant he does. Yes, you want to see the rest of the retrieve, but trust me...click!

8. Repeat #7 until the dog is racing out to get the dumbbell. Then proceed to add the turn back into your little chain.

9. Work as above with the dumbbell being placed on the floor a giant step in front of the dog. Delay R+ for just a moment after he performs the TAKE, giving him a chance to start the turn that was shaped a few lessons ago.

10. Clicking early into the turn will cause it to become tight, so don't wait until he is turned completely around before clicking. If he gets lazy about the turn, making it wider than necessary, just turn around and run away a few steps, while reminding yourself to work on clicking sooner.

11. As you work the turn, click only the tight ones and ignore the rest. A tight turn will give him cause to give a fast return. You can let the dog know the turn wasn't tight enough, but I don't recommend it; just start over.

SHAPING A FAST RETURN – LESSON 19

1. Further raise the distance criterion by taking a step back as he makes the turn and R+ him for coming fast out of the turn.

2. Continue taking one step back until the dog is hurrying to catch up to you, but R+ before he does. Let the dumbbell fall to the ground - do not try to catch it - and pick it up before feeding the treat.

3. Repeat until you can see the dog anticipating that you are going to move back by quickly turning and moving toward you.

4. Repeat this less until the dog is turning fast and bouncing back to you, even though he is still traveling just a few steps.

ADDING THE THROW – LESSON 20

If the dog has been shaped through all of the behaviors up to this point, this will just be a fun lesson for you both.

1.   While holding the dog – hold him whether he knows how to stay or not so you don't set him up for failure by making him break a STAY – toss the dumbbell out a few feet in front of him.

2.   Immediately send him with your TAKE command and be sure to release the collar as you say it – we are always building drive.

3.   Allow him to perform a few retrieves as described in #2 before clicking for parts that you like. Jackpot him when he returns. Do NOT ask for FRONTS at this time.

4.   Now, click for anything you like in the retrieve chain; don't be afraid, you won't break it. The dog will drop the dumbbell when you click.

5.   Raise criteria by just standing there, looking at the dropped dumbbell until he goes to retrieve it again. He is now fixing the broken chain.

6.   When you first allow him to restart, click him for getting it again a few times. He is learning the importance of having the dumbbell in his mouth.

7.   Quit after a few of the above and allow some latent learning.

8.   Repeat this entire lesson for at least another session, preferably the next day, before moving on and have <u>fun</u> with it. Don't wear out the dog, as always, but leave him wanting more.

STIMULUS CONTROL – LESSON 21

Having stimulus control over a behavior means:

✓   The dog will not anticipate and perform it before receiving the command

✓   He will not refuse to perform the behavior when commanded to do so

✓   He will not perform it when a different behavior is requested

✓   He will perform it correctly even when distractions are present.

✓   He will wait like the dog in Figure 8.

1. Toss the dumbbell a short distance while holding onto the dog's collar. No leash is required in this game.

2. Delay sending him for the dumbbell - this is the start of the STAY command, the start of stimulus control.

3. Give him your TAKE command as you release the collar.

4. Work this shaping game as above for a few times and then raise criteria by not sending him until he stops pulling on the collar. This is the start of shaping him to wait for the TAKE command before rushing forward.

5. Add your STAY command when your dog is showing signs of understanding that he cannot go until he is not pulling on the collar. When he does, remove your hand from the collar, add a short leash (one he can drag, like a drop tab) and continue working while holding on to the drop tab in case of anticipation.

6. If he gets away from you, click him for anything he does that's correct, and get a better hold next time.

7. Add distractions such as toys and people along his path to the dumbbell. There will be no R+ for picking up toys. And going to the people causes them to turn their backs to the dog. You can add a mild aversive if necessary, but it probably won't be.

8. Proofing with food when the behavior is young and tender might put a strain on a dog that has strong food drives. For such a dog I would use a leash so he <u>never</u> gets to the treats so it is <u>never</u> a reinforceable behavior. If he goes for the treats, give your verbal aversive, "ACK!" or "ICKY!" and go get the dumbbell, ending the game for a short time.

SHAPING THE FRONT – LESSON 22

> TRAINER'S NOTE:
>
> Adding the FRONT is a major rise in criteria.
>
> A lowering of standards for both the FRONT and the hold are called for; there is no room for punishment here.
>
> The FRONT behavior must already be shaped and on stimulus control before proceeding with this lesson.

This behavior is shaped without a throw to keep it isolated. You will be adding it in at the tail end of the retrieve chain – back chaining it in.

1. Hold the dog by the collar with your left hand, take a giant step forward, bend forward from the waist, and present the dumbbell at arm's length.

2. Send the dog with your TAKE command.

3. As he turns with the dumbbell, stand straight and call him into FRONT position. If he is a long-bodied dog, you might have to back up a step so he can straighten up.

4. Expect that he will spit out the dumbbell at the sound of your voice or as he sits, for this should be unknown territory to him.

5. Wait and allow him to pick up the dumbbell. Click for the pick up even if he stood up for it. Don't make him sit again.

6. Work at this level, allowing the dog to sort out in his own mind what the expected behavior is. He will soon begin holding through the sit.

7. Click for any sit while holding, taking care to click early, before he spits out. He is learning to hold this position until he hears the click.

8. For a dog that continuously drops the dumbbell before getting to FRONT, grab the dumbbell and run away several steps, then stop and hold it out to your left in a surprise TAKE just as he arrives at HEEL position (not after he sits, but as he arrives). Then quickly back up a few steps causing him to turn and bringing him in close to FRONT (silently, no commands for this). R+ at the moment he arrives at FRONT (without a sit), clarifies for the dog that the FRONT without the dumbbell is now a useless action.

SHAPING THE GIVE – LESSON 23

TRAINER'S NOTE:
This lesson may be paired with the FRONT, but only after the front is fairly solid.

This is where the HOLD is truly taught and learned. Shaping of the GIVE command is what cements the hold for most dogs. Shaped correctly, the GIVE command will in turn shape a secure hold from the moment of pickup all the way to FRONT. Patience and a sense of humor are important on the day you start teaching this exercise.

This is also where a TAKE while sitting in FRONT is handy, since you can just put the dumbbell in his mouth to start each game.

1. Since we are shaping the GIVE rather than the FRONT, sit your dog at heel and pivot out in front of him and into proper FRONT position.

2. Either present the dumbbell from FRONT or give it to him before pivoting into FRONT position. He probably won't hold it, however, from HEEL position, as we haven't shaped it.

3. If the dumbbell is presented to the dog from the FRONT position, do not be surprised if he doesn't understand, since all other TAKES have been to the side or away from the trainer. Shaping it will give you the opportunity to shape a new behavior on your own. Do not continue with the GIVE until he is fluently accepting the dumbbell from FRONT position.

4. With your dog positioned in FRONT and holding the dumbbell, have both hands at your sides, as they were during the FRONT shaping.

5. Slowly move one hand slowly toward the dumbbell or just wiggle your fingers and be ready for the dog to spit out or to begin mouthing as a nervous gesture.

6. This is a HUGE rise in the picture criterion for the dog – you haven't behaved so rudely in the past.

7. When he mouths the dumbbell, remember how close your hand got before he mouthed.

62

8. Move your hand again but this time do less movement or travel a shorter distance than the last time.

9. R+ if he does not mouth or drop the dumbbell. Of course he'll drop it at the click. Pick it up to restart the game. Do NOT allow him to pick it up.

10. Stay at this level until the dog sits quietly, waiting for the click, until you are able to move both hands, getting closer with first one, then the other, then both simultaneously.

11. Build up to touching the dumbbell with just one finger. If you can, jackpot the dog and quit for several minutes or until the next shaping session.

12. When you resume, quickly touch one bell with one finger, which is where you left off. If he does not allow this, lower criteria to just moving your hands and work up to the touch.

13. Continue to raise the touch criteria until you can place one hand on one bell of the dumbbell. Before attempting to touch the other bell with the other hand, work until you can tug a little on the dumbbell with one hand.

14. The same shaping process used for the first hand must be repeated for the second, although it will proceed more smoothly and quickly because the dog now has general knowledge about touching of the dumbbell.

15. Move both hands towards the dumbbell and R+ each time you get closer than the time before. If he mouths at this point, just put your hands back at your sides and start over. Don't give any type of aversive other than leaving him sitting there and holding.

16. When both hands can touch both bells at the same time without any mouthing, push and pull gently against them, clicking the dog for not reacting.

17. So far we haven't given any command to GIVE the dumbbell, working strictly on holding it while we touch it.

18. Introducing the GIVE command is going to be as easy as it gets, because he'll spit out the dumbbell as soon as you say it. It constitutes a click in his mind and substitutes the clicker as the release command.

19. If the dog gets up after or while giving, you may command him to SIT before giving him any R+ or just wait for him to offer the SIT. Click the first couple of SITS whether offered or commanded.

TRAINER'S NOTE:

In a proper GIVE the trainer's hands remain still while the dog opens his mouth then backs his head away from the dumbbell. This is accomplished by not moving your hands after the GIVE command, but holding the dumbbell still, which forces the dog to back his head away from it. R+ should come after the head is backed away.

3 - 4 RETRIEVE PROBLEMS

IN THE RING – LESSON 24

Any dog can have retrieve "accidents." His level of reliability will increase as his trainer increases his amount of practice, reinforcing him at the appropriate times. Increase the dog's understanding and you decrease the occurrence of retrieve accidents. Usual retrieve problems in the obedience ring include:

- ✓ Distracting scents in the grass or on the mat.
- ✓ Ringside distractions.
- ✓ Loud noises or scary noises.
- ✓ Poor lighting or throwing into the sun (the latter falls under poor judging).
- ✓ Tall grass –more of a problem for toy breeds.
- ✓ Poor dumbbell tossing.
- ✓ A missed command, common in buildings with echoes.

As the dog performs the retrieve under a variety of conditions, his failure rate will diminish to almost zero. He is still, however, at the mercy of poor throws and poor commands from his handler. Practice throwing your different dumbbells on all sorts of surfaces; a hoop target helps. It is a good idea for the serious competitor to have different dumbbells for grass, for asphalt, and for thin and thick matting.

If there is a lot of noise or a lot of echo, be sure to give your command loud enough for him to hear you. My extremely reliable dog missed a softly spoken TAKE command on scent articles one time – flunk.

Here's one more important note – in following these lessons you have shaped your dog to turn to the right after picking up the dumbbell. It stands to reason that if you are going to throw crooked, always throw a little to the left. This is especially important on the Retrieve over High Jump exercise.

When a throw is too far to the right, and the dog turns to the right, he can be looking directly at the handler after the turn; the jump isn't even in the picture. Chances are this dog will return to the handler without going over the jump. Proof for this very problem by making deliberately crooked throws, which will help, but in the ring everyone is a little stiffer, including the dog.

> TRAINER'S NOTE:
>
> If you make a crooked throw, the worst thing you can then do is look at the dog and think about him not taking the jump. Instead, look directly at the jump and visualize your dog as he looks flying over it and carrying the dumbbell. If you do, he might see you looking there, look there himself, remember the jump, and your visualization will come true.

There are "rules" that go along with throwing the dumbbell for your dog and issuing the retrieve command. They are:

✓ Toss the dumbbell a little to the left of center. This is especially important when performing retrieves over the high jump.

✓ Throw the dumbbell far out, right to the ring barrier. This decreases the dog's chance of missing the jump on his way back to FRONT.

✓ When showing on dark matting, use a light colored dumbbell and when on light carpet use one that is dark or unpainted.

✓ Be sure to practice both your throws and your dog's retrieves on a new dumbbell before taking it into the ring. I threw a new dumbbell once and my dog did a smart retrieve, but had a scowl on her face as she returned with the dumbbell. About 3 feet from FRONT position, she spat the dumbbell out at my feet, then came smartly into FRONT. It was cute and I deserved it, but it cost 3 points for dropping.

✓ Give your dog clear commands (use something like "Take It" for a flat retrieve and "Over" or "Jump" for retrieves over the high jump).

✓ Proof against incorrect TAKES - described below.

Traveling Beyond the Dumbbell

If your dog begins the habit of traveling past the dumbbell and turning before picking up, you will need to break the chain down to this point by clicking him as soon as his head drops toward the dumbbell to look at it on his way past, but before he moves beyond it. It should cause him to abort the retrieve and return for the treat. After feeding him you may allow him to restart the exercise and then click him for picking up.

After several clicks for looking at the dumbbell, he will probably go to the dumbbell and look at you, anticipating the click. Just wait for him to continue the exercise. This is a lesson that can help to cement for him what the retrieve is all about. By allowing him to think it through, he will become stronger at it.

A more mechanical way of fixing this problem is to throw the dumbbell against a wall for a while and click early, when he starts his TAKE.

Not Picking up the Dumbbell

Another response he may give is to approach the dumbbell without even looking at it, and then run back to you for some sort of help or in anticipation of the click. Quietly watch and enjoy how your dog works through it. He will try many things including snatching the dumbbell quickly in an effort to get you to click. Clicking this offered behavior will speed up the overall retrieve as well as helping to overcome the problem.

The only time I've seen a dog that has been shaped by these methods refuse to bring back the dumbbell was a dog that had been corrected by his impatient trainer the day before because he didn't wait for the TAKE command. We just lowered all criteria by throwing and sending the dog while the dumbbell was in the air, making it a play retrieve. He loosened up, forgave his trainer, and starting retrieving normally again.

Incorrect Throws

Bad dumbbell throwing can cause several problems, but the main one is a crooked front. Thoroughly proof the dog in handling really crooked throws by deliberately throwing at acute angles and clicking him for straightening himself up. Props can be used to help him understand this process; pieces of 4x4's indicating front can help, but must be faded through the use of smaller targets until no target is required.

Also, practice, practice, and then practice more at throwing your dumbbells so they will go as straight as possible and as far as required.

"Funny" Dumbbells

The almost square dumbbells designed for dogs with narrow muzzles present challenges for both exhibitors and dogs. When thrown they flip along and often land on end. Even dumbbells with longer mouthpieces and shorter ends will occasionally land on end. For this reason, it is recommended that you teach your dog how to pick up a sideways dumbbell.

If not taught how to properly pick up a dumbbell when it's on end, most dogs will push it over with a paw, resulting in a big point loss for playing with it.

To shape the sideways retrieve, go back to the take from hand, standing and offering the dumbbell at an arm's length away. Hold the dumbbell at an angle perpendicular to the ground and send your dog with a TAKE command.

Figure 16 – Taking Dumbbells on End
Dumbbells land on end at times, making it a good idea to shape a take with the dumbbell on end. This puppy doesn't know how to turn his head for the take of an upended dumbbell, so is pouncing it instead.

Figure 18 shows a dog not shaped specifically in how to retrieve a dumbbell that has landed on its end. He's stepping on the dumbbell and will pick it up by the bell or push it over with his paw; both cause point deductions.

"BAD" TAKE HABITS – LESSON 25

When dogs are taught the TAKE from FRONT position rather than from HEEL position, they often develop retrieve problems involving the TAKE behavior. When you keep in mind that dogs are picture and position-oriented animals, the reason behind this is easy to see.

When a dog is used to seeing his trainer behind the dumbbell as he takes it in his mouth, he will often go past a thrown dumbbell, make his turn, then perform the TAKE on the way back. This gives him the picture as it has been for reinforcement. AKC Obedience Regulations state that the dog "shall go directly to the dumbbell, pick it up, and return directly to the handler."

If you are correcting this bad behavior because you shaped the TAKE from FRONT position, cover all the TAKE lessons in this book. Click early to show the dog how important it is to TAKE on the way out and during the turn rather than after the turn.

MOUTHING THE DUMBBELL – LESSON 26

There are many fully trained dogs competing with less than perfect TAKES, holds, and returns, but mouthing can cause a dog to accidentally drop the dumbbell. Some drop the dumbbell on purpose so they can pounce on it and "catch" it again before having to give it up. They still pass, but lose points. Here are some ideas to overcome mouthing problems.

If your already trained retriever is mouthing, work this book's lessons to re-shape your TAKE. Click early to avoid retraining the same problem.

Make sure your dog's dumbbells are sized to properly fit his mouth, that they are not too heavy for him, and that he doesn't have a tooth problem.

SLOW RETURNS – LESSON 27

Slow returns are usually a sign of hesitation; dogs that have been corrected for crooked FRONTS demonstrate this behavior, especially in the last few steps to the handler.

To solve this problem, there are many things to do. First, perform all the TAKE lessons in this book where moving several steps backward after the TAKE is required. This adds a little chase to the retrieve game and most dogs will join in.

You can try doing some chase recalls to speed up a wary dog, run backwards a few steps, or toss a treat between you legs, allowing him to go beyond FRONT position to get to it. Do this without the dumbbell at first, and then add the dumbbell into the games using TAKES from your hand. Eventually, throw short retrieves and reshape the FRONT using the above games of turning and running away, rushing backward several steps, and tossing treats beyond FRONT position, alternating from one to the other until he feels good about coming into FRONT.

Don't put pressure on the dog for a perfect FRONT until you have a perfect retrieve, and work the FRONTS separately. FRONTS are what happen after the retrieve, so get the retrieve, then get the FRONT , then put them together.

Here's one more way of getting a fast return. Click the dog as soon as he completes the turn. He will rush back to get to the treat. You can give a KGS (keep going signal) while he is running fast, and even click him again. He is probably coming without the dumbbell, but as he becomes fluent at carrying he will choose to carry it farther and farther, until he gets over his slowness.

3 - 5 DIRECTED RETRIEVE

The Directed Retrieve is a required exercise in the AKC Utility class. It involves three white cotton gloves that are placed 30" in from one end of the ring. Two of the gloves are placed in the opposite corners 30" in from the side barriers and the third is placed in the center, between the other two. The dog and handler stand near the center of the ring with their backs to the gloves as a ring steward places them on the floor. The center glove is directly behind the dog and handler.

Glove positions are indicated by number: Glove #1 is over the handler's right shoulder, Glove #2 is directly behind the handler, and Glove #3 is over the handler's left shoulder. It is customary, but not required that the dog and handler pivot to the left to retrieve the #3 glove – Figure 18.

After the gloves are properly placed and the judge determines that the dog and handler team is ready, he instructs the handler to retrieve a glove, identifying which glove by its position number. Some judges also point in the direction of the designated glove, making it easier on the handler to determine which way to pivot.

The handler and dog are required to pivot smartly toward the designated glove. At the end of the pivot the dog sits, and the handler marks the glove with a hand signal as he gives the dog a verbal retrieve command. The dog must go directly to the designated glove, retrieve it, return directly to the handler, and perform a FRONT and hold until told to GIVE.

Because the previously taught obedience retrieve is now general knowledge to your dog, the stationary glove retrieve will not present many problems. As with the dumbbell retrieve, all individual behaviors in the directed retrieve chain should be reinforced and those that can should be put on stimulus control before chaining them together. Because the glove is dry and unpleasant in the dog's mouth, the TAKE, turn, and hold benefit from heavy reinforcement.

Problem areas usually occur in the pivot (a HEELing issue), choosing the correct glove, and playing with the glove during the TAKE or the return. Each of these behaviors should be worked separately, outside the chain, to help prevent these problems from occurring in the ring.

Choosing the wrong glove is the most common reason for failure to pass the Directed Retrieve exercise. The following lessons, if followed, will shape your dog into getting the correct glove, and return with it without shaking it like a toy.

SCORING THE UTILITY CLASS – DIRECTED RETRIEVE

The American Kennel Club (AKC) Obedience Regulations, <u>Utility Exercises and Scores</u>, state that the Utility class exercises and maximum scores are:

1. Signal Exercise   40 points

2. Scent Discrimination Article No. 1   30 points

3. Scent Discrimination Article No. 2   30 points

4. Directed Retrieve   30 points

5. Moving Stand and Examination   30 points

6. Directed Jumping   40 points

Maximum Total Score .... 200 points

To fully understand the allowable commands and signals as required by the AKC for the Directed Retrieve exercise, refer to the Obedience Regulations booklet, which is free of charge upon request.

THE MARKING GAME – LESSON 28

In addition to being able to perform all of the behaviors that make up a retrieve chain, the Directed Retrieve requires that the dog also be able to target and then travel along a direction specified by his handler's hand and arm signal.

Remember the Get It Game from the first section of this book? Here it is again, but this time we are marking to gloves and using a hand signal to indicate the dog's path. This hand signal can be added to the beginning, when the game is initially being shaped, with puppies as young as 10 to 12 weeks old.

Start this game by outfitting your dog with a non-corrective collar (not prong or choke), and then follow these steps:

1. Have the dog on a short leash in the stance of his choice, and on your left (heel position).

2. Do not make demands as to whether he is sitting or standing, as it is not a part of the game at this time.

Shaping the Hand Signal

1. Give your Mark command and toss a treat.

2. Switch hands so that you are now holding him intently in the direction of the treat.

3. Signal the direction with your left hand and arm as in Figure 17.

4. If necessary, you may bend at the knee to get your arm as low as necessary and to maintain your balance.

5. AKC rules allow this bending at the knee only if the dog's size requires it. They also state this is to be a single-movement signal; you cannot swing or jab your arm in the direction of the glove. You must present the signal to the dog, hold it for just a moment, and then remove it.

6. Send the dog using your TAKE command.

7. Raise the directional criterion by tossing the treat at angles then signaling him to travel the line or direction of your left arm.

8. Toss the treat to the same angles, as the gloves will be at in the Utility ring. Further raise directional criterion by placing rather than tossing large treats without the dog present. Click the dog for lining up his head with the hand signal and looking at the target and then send him. Click him again when he gets there then call him back.

Figure 17 – Directed Retrieve Hand Signal
Use your entire arm so your hand is out in front where the dog can see it. This dog is being sent to Glove #1.

69

9.   Increase criteria by delaying the click and getting an implied wait as you did earlier when shaping the Get It Game.

Introducing the Gloves

There are several schools of thought on how to start the glove portion of this exercise and most work equally well.

I prefer to first introduce the glove as a tug toy. I teach the dog to grab it on command, to retrieve it from short distances, and to carry it back to me, all done in a play atmosphere without any clicking, but with much delight and heavy jackpots.

I also use the glove in conjunction with another game that is useful in teaching not to play with an object unless told to. The game is not covered in this workbook, but the purpose behind it is to give a light-switch type of control over the dog's play times. The cues to start playing on command and quit playing on command later become cues for work on command and to quit working on command. By using the glove in this game the dog learns that it is a play object if the trainer says it is and is a work object otherwise.

One advantage of playing tug and retrieve games with the gloves is that they help to get the dog over the dryness and texture of the glove, which many do not like.

Placing a tennis ball inside each glove enables them to be thrown in play retrieves with a level of accuracy that cannot be achieved with an empty glove. Clicking the dog for fast retrieves, tight turns, and so on during play sessions helps build drive when the pressure is on to play by rules and to work. For instance, throwing a play retrieve while holding the dog, and then sending and releasing him before the glove stops moving, increases drive. He can be clicked for jumping out to get it and for making a fast grab. Never mind that he stops the retrieve and returns for his treat...without drive it won't matter much how the rest of this exercise looks.

Tight turns are really important in this exercise. The other gloves on the ground are an enticement for the dog and can lure him away as he makes his turn back to you. Reinforce tight turns by clicking early after the TAKE and also by playing a fronting game where you call him and then run away a few steps. Jackpot him when he turns fast to get to you.

Mixing up play and work is a good way to build drive, too. A FRONT can be requested as the dog is returning from a play retrieve, treats can be tossed through the trainer's legs during the "real" thing, the GIVE command may be worked, or another glove may be tossed as this one is being returned to the trainer.

Many trainers start out with only Gloves # 1 and #3, training at that level until the dog is reliable at either. I like to start with all three, but positioned differently than they are in the obedience ring.

The Pivot

The dog is pivoted from a position with his back to the gloves into a position facing the designated glove. This a HEELing exercise and is not covered in this book.

Any dog that does not fully understand the directed retrieve hand signal will be less reliable at getting the correct glove than one that does. There is always the chance that a dog will end up in a crooked position after the pivot and be facing the wrong glove. The chance that he will take the wrong glove in this situation is reduced if he understands how to travel in the direction of the hand signal.

- ✓ A dog that over pivots for Glove #1 is likely to go to Glove #2 since that's the glove he is facing.

- ✓ Under pivoting for Glove #2 will face him toward Glove #1.

- ✓ A dog that over pivots to Glove #3 in a left pivot, is likely to mistakenly bring back Glove #2.

From the above examples, it is easy to see the importance of a utility dog being able to follow a signal rather than just following his nose.

Sending the Dog

Start with your gloves at least 20' apart with Glove #2 about 10 feet away from your center position – Figure 18. Have your dog on a leash or line (not a retractable lead) long enough for the dog to reach the glove, but one that will allow you to stop his forward motion should he travel toward the wrong glove.

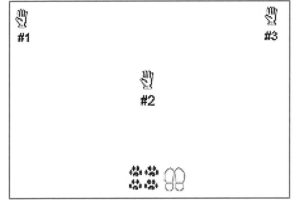

Figure 18 – Glove placement for shaping the Directed Retrieve. Glove #2 is about 10' in front of the dog. Glove #2's closeness helps the dog to discern between the gloves.

Proceed as outlined below:

1. Start with your dog sitting in heel position, outfitted with a non-corrective collar and a leash long enough to reach to any of your placed gloves.

2. With you both facing Glove #2, give him a hand signal to Glove #1. This may require that your arm come into contact with your dog's face before his head turns; that's okay for now.

3. R+ any head turn he makes to follow the line of your hand signal.

4. Repeat #1 and #2, alternating between Gloves #1 and #3, but always facing Glove #2.

5. Continue to work steps #1 and #2 until the dog can reliably look in the direction designated.

6. When your dog can consistently look in the direction of the hand signal, send him to first Glove #1, then Glove #3, alternating between those two gloves.

7. If he seems to have a problem in going to the correct glove, move your dog closer to Glove #2.

8. R+ for any and all portions of the send, the retrieve, the turn, the return, or the delivery that is to your liking, breaking the chain time and time again at different intervals.

9. Add the FRONT if you feel comfortable about the hold, but you may still toss treats between your legs to increase drive (be sure to wait until the dog is within a couple of steps before spreading your legs and tossing the treat). The dog will drop the glove, eat the treat, and, if you do nothing, he should pick the glove up and come to FRONT.

10. Allow the dog to restart this exercise if he has at all been squeamish about holding the dry glove or performing a FRONT while carrying it.

Getting the Correct Glove

TRAINER'S NOTE:

Not sending your dog to Glove #2 at this time is teaching him to ignore it even though it is closer and directly in front of him.

Most dogs fail this exercise because they retrieve Glove #2 regardless of where they were sent.

7. As the dog becomes reliable at avoiding Glove #2 and moving out in the direction marked, start sending him to Glove #2.

11. Send him to Gloves #1 and #3 twice as often as you send to Glove #2.

12. All you and your dog need now is practice and distractions.

13. Work all parts of the directed retrieve on many objects, like toys, his leash, and your purse.

14. Work on the FRONT and GIVE portions separately and within the chain.

15. I have found most dogs to be less reliable at holding the glove tightly than the dumbbell.

16. Really driven dogs, however, like Border Collies, don't want to let go of the glove.

17. If your dog doesn't want to let go of the glove, put extra effort into controlling all tug games by reinforcing a quit-on-command behavior.

Proofing the Directed Retrieve

I like to practice this exercise and also proof it by tossing a glove in the direction the dog is facing; here's where a tennis ball in the glove is handy. I then give a directional signal to a different glove and send the dog to it.

<u>**Scoring the Directed Retrieve**</u>

Point deductions listed below are particular only to the Directed Retrieve exercise.

1. The dog will receive a score of zero points for:

2. Any commands or signals by the handler, after turning, to position the dog to face the designated glove.

3. For not going directly to the designated glove.

4. The dog will receive minor to substantial point deductions, depending on the extent for

5. A handler who touches a dog.

6. A handler who uses excessive motions while turning to face the glove.

7. A handler who overturns to face the glove.

3 - 6 SCENT ARTICLES

Scent Discrimination is an AKC Utility exercise with a high point value. It starts with 10 articles, five made of metal and five made of leather. They can be almost anything, but most exhibitors use articles shaped like dumbbells. A number stamped or printed on it in an area that makes it easy to read identifies each article.

Upon entering the Utility ring or just prior to the Scent Discrimination exercise, the judge or exhibitor selects one metal and one leather article – both with the same number. At the start of the exercise the remaining eight articles are placed on the floor about 20' in front of the dog and exhibitor.

When the articles have been placed on the floor, both dog and handler turn their backs to the "pile" of articles and the exhibitor places his scent on one of the previously selected two articles by touching the article with one or both hands. Upon request from the judge the exhibitor turns over the article and the judge then positions the scented article in the pile next to the unscented articles. The judge then instructs the exhibitor to send his dog.

It is at the exhibitor's discretion whether he holds his hand out to give the scent to the dog before sending him. After giving the scent the exhibitor either pivots and waits for the dog to sit and then sends him, or he sends the dog as they pivot, in which case the dog will not sit but will instead go directly to the article pile.

The dog must go directly to the pile, "work" the pile for as long as it takes him to scent the articles, then selects and picks up the correct article. He then returns to FRONT position and holds the article until told to GIVE it. The entire process is then repeated for the second article. The scenting and retrieving of each article is scored separately.

Scenting is one of those things that dogs do so well, we can't really tell or show them how to do it. What we can do is to set up a scent routine and R+ the dog for showing interest, for attempting to scent, then for scenting correctly. For a dog that already knows the retrieve, we need only to set up a game that will entice the dog to scent, and then adequately reward his effort.

I find tie down boards and strings that tie scent articles together to be cumbersome because they involve crutches that later have to be faded and can cause behaviors that need re-shaping as training progresses. However, this is the method most trainers use and they are successful at using it.

SCORING THE UTILITY CLASS – SCENT DISCRIMINATION

The American Kennel Club (AKC) Obedience Regulations, <u>Utility Exercises and Scores</u>, state that the Utility class exercises and maximum scores are:

1. Signal Exercise   40 points

2. Scent Discrimination Article No. 1   30 points

3. Scent Discrimination Article No. 2   30 points

4. Directed Retrieve   30 points

5. Moving Stand and Examination   30 points

6. Directed Jumping   40 points

Maximum Total Score .... 200 points

To fully understand the allowable commands and signals as required by the AKC for the Scent Discrimination exercise, refer to the Obedience Regulations booklet, which is free of charge upon request.

PUPPY SCENTING GAMES – LESSON 29

A fun game that teaches a puppy to use his scenting ability on command is to drop a small piece of tasty treat into a shallow box of shredded paper. Click the puppy when he is obviously sniffing, causing him to stop sniffing and come for a treat. He can then remember what he was doing and return to the box to continue his search. Sniffing is not only clicked, but is also self-reinforcing; since he eats the treat after he locates it with his nose.

Using a hard biscuit enables the trainer to click when he hears the crunching sound that tells her the puppy found it. He might just drop the biscuit and come for a treat and then go back for the biscuit. Raise criteria by dropping the treats into his toy box.

Alternate between allowing the behavior to be self-reinforcing by making the treat the primary reinforcement and clicking him for searching by scent alone. If he is clicked, he will receive two treats – they were both earned.

ADDING THE FIND IT COMMAND – LESSON 30

When he will work diligently through the shredded paper and through his toy box, he understands the scenting game. Raise criteria by restraining him and adding the "Find It" command, letting him go as you say it. Play this game for a short time and then raise criteria again.

Substitute the treat with a favorite toy that belongs to the puppy. This teaches him that not all finds are for treats. With this rise in criteria go back to clicking for merely sniffing in the box, then for finding the toy, then for picking it up, and so on.

74

If this puppy is hot to play this game, introduce a metal scent article that is lightweight, easy for him to carry, and is easy to pull out of the toy box, too. A canning lid works well. I scent it heavily with a familiar scent like hot dog juice.

Raise criteria by hiding the scent article in the house – in a laundry basket, under a chair, behind his toy box, and so on. Hiding his eyes as you place it or putting him in another room will further raise criteria.

Alternate the games between easy and difficult hiding places, and then easy again. To make sure he has opportunities for easy wins where he doesn't have to work as hard.

Up to this point he has not been required to retrieve the article, only to find it by using its scent.

BUILDING DRIVE TO SCENT AND RETRIEVE – LESSON 31

> TRAINER'S NOTE:
> Putting pressure on the dog to find or to retrieve will return disastrous results, which can be seen in the obedience ring at every trial. Too many dogs are frightened of the scenting exercise because of the pressure that has been put upon them to *get it right*.

When the dog is keen on the scenting game and will pick up metal articles, I play the game while watching TV, straightening up the house, or getting ready for work. That this isn't just a mechanical retrieve as previously shaped, but has many variables, can make trainers nervous and dogs even more nervous.

In the obedience ring the dog is given as much time to find the correct article as needed. As long as he continues to work, he will be allowed to do so. Seemingly not paying attention and allowing him to go about his task relieves all pressure on him to work. He will work because he wants to.

I gradually raise criteria by hiding articles in baskets of laundry and under couch cushions. He will begin retrieving on his own as I further raise criteria by delaying the click. After all, how else will he be able to show me that he has located what he was sent for?

It becomes a wonderful game that he controls by going faster and faster with his run, his sniffing, and his return with the article. He raises his own criteria because he is the one determining the rules -- he is the trainer, while I'm washing dishes! I add leather articles only after the dog is desensitized to carrying a hard metal article.

When the dog knows enough about the game to consistently FIND an article by scent, he is ready for some "real" scent discrimination shaping.

There are many variations to this process. The two I use are not widely used, but I like them and have been successful in using them.

Method #1

First I go back to the old game of hiding a scented article under my chair or another easy area, but have unscented articles in plain view and close by, like on the floor in front of me while I watch television.

The dog now knows what the articles look like and he will pick up one of those on the floor close by. I ignore this behavior entirely. No matter how many he picks up, I ignore him. He eventually goes searching for the scented article and is clicked for finding it, then for retrieving it.

I build this up until I can place the scented article in the pile with the rest and he will find it. I add leather articles only after he can scent the metal. Leather is easier for most dogs to pick up, but presents scenting problems because it carries a scent of its own.

With all the unscented articles at my feet, leather included, I add a scented leather article in an easy to find place, like under the chair. He might return to just grabbing articles, but when ignored will search out the scented one.

Eventually, I put them all in a pile, use the command to find the scented article, and we're done shaping this portion of the exercise.

Method #2

I scent ALL the articles and put them all on the floor, arranged much as they would be in the utility class.

Since he has a 100% chance of being correct, failure isn't an issue. During this early shaping process I click for the FIND and for the retrieve, sometimes individually, sometimes as a chain. I wait to see if he will restart the exercise on his own by picking up the article after eating the treat. If he does, he gets clicked for that, too.

I begin to add unscented articles and allow him to choose incorrectly and receive no reinforcement for it as in Method #1. He will soon realize he must scent as he did in the earlier games and be able to find the correct one.

Eventually there is only one scented article. When he can consistently find it, this portion of the shaping is over.

THE ARTICLE PILE – LESSON 33

Figure 19 – Scenting the Pile
By using the "everything scented" method the dog learns to sniff every article even if has air-scented the correct one. This puppy new to scenting but is doing a good job of sniffing. It's the #2 leather next to his left front foot.

Figure 20 – Taking the Scent Article
The puppy makes the correct decision and starts back with the article, but not without hesitation as shows in how he is carrying. Just after this he carried it back to the pile to double-check. Allow your dog to re-check the pile until he gains confidence.

All dogs have their own style or pattern for working the article pile. Study your dog's approach to the pile, usually from the left to right, going to the far side and scenting back. Many dogs take this route as they air scent, looking like they are not even interested, and suddenly grab the right article. Most, however, take more time and study the pile to make sure they get it right.

When you have studied your dog's approach, make his practices easier or more difficult by positioning the scented article in his path or where he normally stands to scent the pile.

Once working the pile, click for good decisions, for tight turns, for fast returns, and so on, breaking the chain here and there to build up these different behaviors.

Raising criteria will include placing the articles farther apart, closer together, in a line or cross configuration, and with distractions. I know trainers who use dozens of articles, but since the dog never has to work more than nine articles, I normally use just the nine articles.

PROOFING FOR SCENT DISCRIMINATION – LESSON 34

Distraction is one of those things that can make a good working dog suddenly stop scenting. As previously stated, this isn't one of those behavior chains that can be automated, but requires the dog to stop performing right in the middle of the chain, and think.

Smells on the mat, the judge's aftershave, noise from the audience, tall grass, diving birds, and a dumbbell thrown in an adjoining ring, are all distractions that can result in a zero score.

In a Utility class once my dog Mellie turned from the article pile with the correct metal article sort of hanging off one canine. The look on my face, one of amazement, caused her to go back to the pile, drop the correct article, and bring back an incorrect article. Her face told me she knew it was the wrong one, but also that she felt pushed into it. I made it a point after that to smile through all obedience exercises regardless of what my dog did.

Practice the scent discrimination exercise in tall grass, on cement, and around distractions. You may add other articles such as a favorite toy or a bouncing ball. Use your imagination to come up with distractions to work through.

WHEN THE DOG IS WRONG – LESSON 35

First of all, dogs are never really wrong…they just make mistakes. When a dog makes mistakes in the execution of any behavior, it's probably because he didn't really understand the behavior in the first place. Paired with the pressures of the obedience ring, any lack of understanding is bound to result in failure of some sort. To prevent failure, proof, reinforce, and pay attention. Dogs will indicate their confidence or lack of confidence in how they perform under pressure. If a dog is nervous, goes slowly to the pile, refuses to come back with the article even after picking it up, he's worried. Go back and work each area he shows worry over and keep it light with a lot of play breaks and praise.

Because you now have a creative clicker-trained dog, corrections will be easy. If your dog happens to pick up an incorrect article, simply stand still and <u>wait</u> for him to realize something is wrong. You may point back to the pile if you want an active role, but it isn't necessary.

Allow the dog to return to the pile to conduct a new search for the correct article. If he is carrying the incorrect article, he won't know what to do with it when he locates the correct one, so click him if he acknowledges the correct article. Clicking him for scenting the correct article even though he has already picked up the wrong one will give him the courage and confidence to change his mind if in doubt.

It's important not to react too harshly when an incorrect article is chosen; this is a scenting exercise and not a retrieving exercise. Who's to say he didn't scent the right one and then accidentally grab the wrong one next to it? It is best to just wait and allow the dog to correct his own mistake.

SCENT DISCRIMINATION POINT DEDUCTIONS

The two scent articles are scored separately, each worth 30 points, as show in the AKC point breakdown in Section 2.

Standard deductions will apply for slowness and crookedness, the same as in all AKC recalls and retrieves.

The deductions below are for the Scent Discrimination exercise.

1. The dog will receive a score of zero (he fails to pass) for:

✓ Not going directly to the article pile.

✓ Retrieving the wrong article.

✓ Failure to bring the correct article to the handler.

2. There will be a substantial point deduction (3 points or more) for:

✓ A dog that picks up the wrong article, even though he puts it down immediately.

✓ Any roughness by the handler in imparting his scent to the dog

✓ The handler not turning in place.

3. There will be minor or substantial point deductions for:

✓ A slow or inattentive dog.

✓ A dog not going directly to the articles

✓ A dog not working continuously, scenting the pile

✓ Excessive motions by the handler in turning to face the articles

The AKC Obedience Regulations also state, "There will be no penalty for a dog that takes a reasonably long time examining the articles provided the dog works smartly and continuously." So, don't rush the dog. Instead be happy if your have one that really wants to be sure he's correct before making his selection.

3 - 7 RETRIEVING FOR FLYBALL

Flyball is as much a catching and jumping sport as it is a retrieving sport. Rather than being sent to a dumbbell that has been thrown and now lies in either plain site of on the other side of a solid high-jump, the dog is sent over four low jumps ("hurdles") to retrieve a tennis ball that is embedded in a hole on a box that is located about the same distance away as the thrown dumbbell.

After leaving his handler and jumping the hurdles, the dog arrives at a tennis ball-dispensing contraption and must "flip a switch" that dispenses the ball. He then catches the ball, and returns over the hurdles to the handler with the ball in his mouth. The switch he flips is the front of the box that holds the ball, which is triggered by the weight of the dog's feet landing on it.

Because the ball is propelled forward by the mechanism within the box, that the dog understands how to catch is important. Learning to catch in this case doesn't do much more than accustom him to holding open his mouth so something can to enter it. Fast and efficient Flyball dogs don't catch the ball, but rather position their open mouths over the hole and wait for the ball to spring out.

Work on teaching your dog to catch separately from the retrieve portion of the exercise.

Follow this book's lessons, substituting the dumbbell with a tennis ball until he can retrieve as reliably as if he were training for obedience. Don't slack off on the GIVE behavior, so your dog doesn't develop a habit of sliding around you and returning to the hurdles, which are very fun obstacles.

Since there is little time for fronting behaviors in a Flyball game, substitute the FRONT lessons with food thrown between your legs (behind you) to shape the dog not to slow down as he reaches front position when your legs are open in an A-frame position.

If you plan to also compete in obedience with your Flyball dog, work fronts and pass-throughs with both dumbbells and balls and add the leg position as a part of the cue for which behavior to offer when he arrives at FRONT position. Legs together will cue him to perform a sit at FRONT, and legs apart will cue him to run through without losing speed. The run-through behavior can later be modified to include a stop in front without the sit.

Areas of importance are that the dog will catch the ball in his mouth without playing with it, that he can carry it while jumping, that he doesn't pay attention to the dogs in the other lanes or they might drop, that he will carry it all the way to the trainer, and that the dog give up the ball when commanded to do so.

To help the dog understand that he should not release the ball until he's reached the end of the course, use the lessons in this book to ensure his understanding that the release comes only: 1) near his trainer; and 2) when he's told to release.

Some dogs have the opposite problem from dropping the ball in that they don't want to give up the ball. To the dog, giving up the ball signals the end of the game, which he will be reluctant to do. If your dog is not willing to give up the ball, it is a behavior deserving of individual attention, which is provided in the GIVE lessons of this book.

Because Flyball is a relay race with several dogs running at once and even more waiting their turns and barking with excitement, distractions run high. Each hurdle and jumping over it while carrying the ball is a distraction. When the excitement starts, the "pull" on a dog to join a dog jumping in another lane can cause him to leave his lane.

Work with the clicker and click the dog early for staying in his own lane while planned distractions are presented to him. Having another dog eating a treat or playing a tug game, throwing a squeaky toy, and food on the floor are all good distractions to set up to teach the dog to ignore.

Clicking the dog for not giving in to the temptations of distractions will cause him to continue his run even faster. Feel free to click the increase in speed and R+ heavily when he comes to you.

Unlike Agility, where accuracy and speed go hand-in-hand, Flyball is more about speed. The course is simple, straight down and back over hurdles, so work speed into the retrieve training as discussed in this book. You won't have to do as much as the lesson includes once the dog understands that he's racing against other dogs. The competition alone will take him to maximum speed.

3 - 8 RETRIEVING FOR SERVICE DOGS

Service dogs are expected to retrieve many items, most of which are not dumbbells. To shape reliable retrieves of many different objects, follow the lessons in this book, paying little attention to scoring information, and add object criteria for each object the dog is expected to retrieve. In some instances, a location criterion will be necessary.

If the dog will be required to retrieve a bottle of pills, for example, the location of the bottle must be included in the list of criteria for shaping it. Separate from the retrieve, the dog should be shaped to go to that area.

The "go to" command is very helpful when one is relying on the help of a service dog. We don't always leave our keys or pill bottles in the same spot, so being able to say, "Go to the kitchen and get…" or "Go to my purse and…" broadens the use of the dog's abilities to retrieve objects for his owner.

To add this increase in the retrieve criteria, the dog must first understand the retrieve process:

✓ That he must pick up what he has been sent for.

✓ That he must deliver that object to a hand or lap.

Shaping the dog to deliver the object to a lap is only slightly different from teaching him to hold until being told to release as with obedience retrievers. Using the same give command as already outlined in the book, place a hand under his chin to catch the falling object. This shapes him to drop the object on command rather than wait for hands to be placed on it.

Use the drop behavior associated with the give command to shape a drop into the lap, into the trash can, from the washer into the dryer, and from the hand into a purse or other type of bag.

Object Discrimination

Again, because service dogs are not just carrying dumbbells, object discrimination is a must. Depending on the dog's situation and the mobility of the owner he serves, he might be required to discriminate between a few or many different objects. This is easier than it sounds.

Follow the steps in this book to get the reliability that is required, and when the dog can retrieve simple objects, begin your object discrimination shaping.

Play the clicker training game by placing several objects on the floor and clicking him for looking at, sniffing, pawing, and picking up, and eventually retrieving a particular object. Play this game two or three times before adding the name for the object, then send him to the object after rearranging the order of all the objects on the floor. When you feel the dog understands the object by name, proof his knowledge by placing it on the floor with all new objects.

Figure 21 – Service Dog Retrieving
Here's my service puppy retrieving a dropped item for the blind lady who runs the local grocery. Even though he doesn't really know her, he readily picked up her dropped object and placed it in her hand.

If the dog will be required to retrieve from table tops, be sure to add the height criterion soon after the dog understands the name, or he will spend precious time searching the floor for his object.

If a retrievable object will not always be in a particular location, add location criterion as soon as the dog can retrieve the object by name. Place the object in the kitchen on a chair, allowing the dog to watch, and then go outside the doorway. Send the dog to the location and the object with a command like, "Kitchen, keys." Most of us say, "Go to the kitchen and get my keys," because the dog will learn that the words "Go to" are directional and the words "get my" are a command.

So the statement, "Go to the kitchen and get my keys," tells the dog there is a location to go to, the location is the kitchen, there is something to get and bring back, and that the object is the key chain.

This section has dealt with how the lessons in this book relate to shaping retrieves on service dogs and how they can be used, but is only a sample of what service dogs can do. A dog's natural ability and desire to take care of us makes him a willing student for fetching, carrying, and dragging objects from pulling off socks to picking up coins on bare floors.

Clicker training is versatile enough that other methods and "tricks" can be paired with it to create extraordinary helper dogs; so much so that an entire book could be written on service dog retrieve training using a clicker.

Until such a book is written, imagination is one the best tools a trainer can use. If it's not too big, too heavy, or too dangerous, a dog can retrieve it.

3 - 9 GOOD NEWS

As you traveled through this workbook shaping takes, turns and fronts, you had good and bad days. You might have even made a few mistakes, but then you worked to correct them. You will still have good and bad days with your dog, but you now have the tools to overcome, or to reinforce and save, any new behaviors he throws your way.

Your dog might – will – act as though he doesn't have a clue on occasion, but temporary setbacks are to be expected regardless of the behaviors being trained or of the method used to train them. He's a dog.

The good news is that with clicker training you can always go back and cover old ground to retrain any weak areas that pop up. More good news is that by following the lessons in this book, you now have an operant dog! These are the most fun dogs that make you laugh and enjoy being your dog's partner.

To keep setbacks from becoming large problems, stay aware of what you are shaping and what your dog is learning. Staying aware that dog training is also trainer training - that the dog is allowed his share of training – you will keep things in perspective when you get unexpected responses. With every response your dog gives that is designed to make you react, just smile, and know that he has successfully learned the training game and is using it on you.

I do hope you and your dog have enjoyed working through the lessons in this book as much as I have enjoyed writing (and reliving) every one of them.

Just one more piece of advice – when in doubt, click early!

CLICK! FOR SUCCESS CONTACT INFORMATION

Websites –

http://www.click-4-success.com

http://www.clickertraining.biz

Author –

Email: dogteacher@click-4-success.com

ACKNOWLEDGEMENTS

Many thanks to the people who helped with this latest book revision:

Shelley Collett, my friend who spent a few hours sitting on the floor, the ground, and the pavement taking pictures.

Super Dogs Sports Center located in Simpsonville, KY for the use of their beautiful training facility.

Wesley Anderson for reading and using the original book to train his dog, encourage me to get the revision published, and then to write a flattering book introduction.

All the people on my email list that helped proof and contributed new information to the book.

Finally, thanks to my best buddy, Australian Shepherd puppy Nemo, who turned one year old the day this book was completed and is a wonderful ambassador for Clicker Training. He's still learning the retrieve game, but was a good sport during hours of posing, and remained happy through 300 pictures, many of which took place under a hot sun.

ABOUT THE AUTHOR

Author Lana Mitchell is a pioneer in utilizing clicker training for competitive obedience, herding and conformation. Her clicker trained dogs have achieved High In Trials in both obedience and herding. After she started clicker training in the 1990s, Lana taught conformation and obedience workshops around the country with Karen Pryor and Gary Wilkes. Currently Lana competes in AKC obedience and herding trials, teaches clicker training classes and workshops for obedience, conformation and herding and is a regular contributor to the *Clicker Journal*. She lives in Louisville Kentucky with her Australian Shepherd "Nemo" and her retired cutting horse "Ky."